Selling Project Management
to Senior Executives:
Framing the Moves That Matter

Selling Project Management to Senior Executives: Framing the Moves That Matter

Janice Thomas, PhD

Connie L. Delisle, PhD

Kam Jugdev, PMP, PhD Candidate

With the Assistance of Pamela Buckle, PhD Student

Project Management Institute

Library of Congress Cataloging-in-Publication Data

Thomas, Janice, 1959–
    Selling project management to senior executives: framing the moves that matter/
    Janice Thomas, Connie L. Delisle, Kam Jugdev; with the assistance of Pamela Buckle.
        p. cm.
    Includes bibliographical references.
    ISBN 1-880410-95-8
      1. Project management. 2. Selling. I. Delisle, Connie L., 1965–II. Jugdev, Kam, 1956–
    III. Project Management Institute. IV. Title.

    HD69.P75 T475 2002
    658.4'04--dc21

2002036748

ISBN: 1-880410-95-8

Published by: Project Management Institute, Inc.
                Four Campus Boulevard
                Newtown Square, Pennsylvania 19073-3299 USA
                Phone: 610-356-4600 or Visit our website: www.pmi.org
                E-mail: pmihq@pmi.org

Cover design: Kate Pechter
Interior design: Dewey Messer

10   9   8   7   6   5   4   3   2

Table of Contents

Acknowledgments

This research report was made possible by the strong vision of the Project Management Institute (PMI®) to advance research in project management. We are deeply indebted to PMI for project support, as well as the PMI Research Program Member Advisory Group (RMAG) for their guidance. In particular, we valued the opportunity to work with key people who are driving project management research forward in PMI: Dr. Lewis M. Gedansky, PMI Research Manager during the execution of this project; Mr. Paul Shaltry, liaison between the research project and the RMAG; the other members of the RMAG; and Eva T. Goldman, PMI Research Associate.

We are grateful to the practitioners, consultants, and executives, as well as the academic community for contributions, interest, and support. For all who helped us by providing resources and interviews, answering surveys, attending lectures, and offering questions, critiques, and confirmations, thank you for the time, ideas, and support. We also sincerely thank the many other organizations that supported this research (Athabasca University, CIO Canada, the Computers in Information Processing Society Canada, ESI-International, Professional Engineers of Ontario, PMI Southern Alberta Chapter, the University of Calgary, and SurveySite).

We have looked intently at the study results and selected what is believed to be the most useful information for readers. These results have been presented to audiences around the world who reinforced the interest in the topic and our belief in the value of what has been accomplished. However, the true value of this study, as with all research, comes ultimately from the ideas and discussions it generates in those who read it. The readers are the people who will judge this work and determine its value in practice and theory. We are receptive to receiving questions and comments.

As researchers know, work of this nature is truly a labor of love. We have worked diligently over the last two years to conduct this research, learning a lot about more topics than we care to enumerate, and overcoming many challenges. To do so, we built a close-knit, virtual project team in which the leadership was shared and conducted across distance and time zones. We have a renewed appreciation for the countless hours of volunteer effort that goes into a research project, the complexity of project management research, and the commitment of any research team. The thought of stimulating discussions and thought-provoking encounters in the years to come, when readers examine this work, drove us forward.

For those who supported us behind the scenes, we thank you for your patience. We could not have done this research without your help.

Executive Summary

Why is it hard to get senior executives and practitioners on the same side regarding the value of project management? Why is it hard to "sell" project management to senior executives? These questions, and other related ones, continue to perplex both practitioners and academics alike. Anecdotal reports focus on identifying best practices and strategies for sellers of project management to "get their foot in the door" and secure "airtime" with busy executives. However, there have been no empirical studies conducted within project management on this topic.

In 1999, the Project Management Institute (PMI®), a professional association, identified the need to study the value of project management. This report represents the results of research into "Best Practices for Communicating the Benefits of Project Management to Senior Executives."

Results from this study suggest that very successful sellers pay attention to the quality of the relationship with the buyer, and engage in processes designed to build that relationship. In addition, they are adept at shifting arguments and using flexible argumentation to deal with business context changes over time. The context (in terms of individual's role in the organization) also plays a part in determining the successful processes and arguments. There are significant differences between very successful project personnel and consultants. Successful project personnel emphasize alignment of project management with corporate strategy and goals and distinct value statements. Successful consultants focus on the buyer-seller relationship. In addition, the very successful consultants make no mention of the importance of using facts and evidence to sell.

Ultimately, senior executives want to understand the benefits project management will provide them in their particular context. This is the challenge. It is not easy to sell project management to senior executives—but it is also not impossible. This research identifies distinct arguments, practices, and processes that are more effective than others, and suggests approaches that can be adapted to individual situations.

This Executive Summary provides highlights from each chapter designed to help you find the sections of the book of most interest to you. We wrote this monograph with several audiences in mind. Project managers and consultants will benefit by reading how successful sellers sell project management, and also by understanding what practices to avoid. Senior executives will appreciate the challenges practitioners face in conducting project management work, as well as how project management can drive strategic projects. Researchers will find a foundational study from which to explore these issues in greater detail.

Chapter 1: Study Background

Chapter 1 places the study into context and provides details of the management of the research project. The primary objective of this study is to understand the processes used by project managers and consultants to sell project management to senior executives. The primary research questions were "Why is it difficult to sell project management to senior executives?" and "How do you successfully sell project management to senior executives?" In particular, we set out to:

- Identify the main arguments put forth to sell (promote) project management to senior executives, or in other words, bring project management to their attention (i.e., "get them on the same side").

- Articulate the effective strategies used to sell project management to senior executives, and identify the specific "best practices" related to the process, arguments, and context of successfully selling project management to senior executives.

In this study, "project management" is defined as the disciplines, methodologies, processes, and standards applied to managing projects in the workplace. "Selling" is defined as promoting and advocating project management to senior executives in an organized manner. Study participants were divided into three groups. "Project personnel" includes all organizational personnel involved in project management, and included team leaders and project control officers up to, and including, program directors. "Consultants" are individuals involved in selling project management services and tools to organizations. "Senior executives" are individuals at the vice president level or higher, that sponsor and/or manage projects in their organizations.

Chapter 2: Theoretical Foundation

The literature review identified concepts of interest that provided the theoretical foundation and shaped data collection. Chapter 2 directs the interested reader to the base literatures explored in developing the foundation of this research.

Parts of the project management, marketing, and organizational science literatures were reviewed. The project management literature included very little work on selling. However, we did come across some sources that emphasized the role of the senior executive and the importance of managing expectations. From the marketing literature on selling to executives, we explored the merits of different selling approaches, particularly the work on relationship selling. Some of the findings from the marketing literature focused on the process of building a buyer-seller relationship, and emphasized the elements of trust and credibility. The organizational science literature provided a theoretical foundation for the study based in organizational sense making theory, which explores how we make sense and interact in the world in terms of our values, attitudes, actions, and interpretations. Sense making theory helps us to understand the nature of the gaps in organizational understanding and the problems that can arise because of them. Organizational theories and empirical findings on bringing strategic issues to the attention of executives were also instrumental in shaping our theory-building process.

Chapter 3: Study Methodology

Chapter 3 documents the research methods used to conduct this study. A two-phase approach was employed. Phase I adopted a small-scale, qualitative grounded theory method. Phase II collected primarily quantitative data through a large-scale, online survey. This chapter allows the reader to understand exactly what was done in each phase and to assess the rigor of the research process.

Phase I

In Phase I, we set out to answer the question, "Why is it difficult to sell project management to senior executives?" We interviewed a total of twenty-five participants—senior managers, project personnel, and consultants—to identify the main themes and patterns involved in the process of selling project management to senior executives. We also unearthed barriers to selling project management, basic strategies used to sell project management, effective selling strategies, and reflections from senior executives on what they are looking for. We analyzed the interview data using a qualitative software analysis tool.

Phase II

In Phase II, we addressed the research question, "How do you successfully sell project management to senior executives?" The questions were based on preliminary findings in Phase I, the literature review, discussions with experts in the field, an examination of previous questionnaires on similar topics, and an online survey instrument. The instrument consisted of 105 items (94 five-point Likert scale items and 11 open-ended, textual questions). SurveySite™ (www.surveysite.com) administered the survey. Three thousand and ninety-three respondents accessed the survey, and we collected a useable sample totaling 1,868 participants for a minimum response rate of 5.3 percent overall. The survey accuracy rate of +/- 2.27 percent (19 times out of 20) means that the questionnaire provided data that is statistically valid. The results did not occur by chance and are reasonably generalizable.

A three-part analysis of this data was conducted. Part One of the analysis involved demographic statistical analysis using Microsoft® Excel® and SPSS® statistical software packages. This approach allowed us to do descriptive analyses. Part Two of the analysis included scrutinizing the data on participant demographics (position, industry, and country) and involved both descriptive and inferential statistics. Part Three of the analysis involved conducting Exploratory Factor Analysis (EFA) to reduce and summarize the data to identify the top factors explaining how project personnel and consultants sell the discipline to senior executives. One-half of the data was used for this EFA analysis. The second half was retained for future testing purposes. Thus, EFA results are based on one-half of the respondents. The other half is retained for further studies that would confirm these findings. On this basis, the sample size was 933. It consisted of 499 project personnel, 244 consultants, and 190 senior executives.

Chapter 4: Phase I Findings: Why Is It Difficult to Sell Project Management to Senior Executives?

Phase I results suggest that while senior executives recognize the importance of project management to their organization, they view it as of importance to the operational or tactical level of the organization. Project management only becomes a strategic or senior management issue when there is a crisis in the market or internally in the organization. Chapter 4 describes the models that were developed to explain this process.

The results indicate that project management remains a tough sell for reasons related to the cognitive gaps between what sellers promote and what purchasers need to hear.

- When project management is purchased during times of crises, practitioners lose credibility, as management may view them as being responsible for project failures.

- Practitioners do not necessarily view selling project management as one of their roles.

- Sellers do not convincingly connect project management to business strategy, thus relegating it to the operational level of the firm (and senior executives are not focused on this level, as they see it as the purview of the middle management).

Chapter 5: Phase II Findings: Demographics and Practice

Chapter 5 presents descriptive statistics on the sample and their responses to an important set of questions about the state of practice of project management. The results suggest that project management is indeed becoming increasingly important and its use is growing in organizations. At the same time, investment in the discipline is quite low, as indicated by the percentage of project personnel receiving little or no formal training. Although, senior executives' expectations of project management as a strategic initiative are believed to be realistic, the appropriate project management methods are not generally being applied. Ultimately this outcome means that strategically important projects are not consistently meeting specification, cost, or schedule expectations. While organizations believe that there are such things as appropriate methods (that is, they know how to manage projects) the results suggest that these organizations are woefully inept in doing that effectively. This "knowing-doing gap" creates a serious contextual challenge that needs to be overcome by those attempting to sell project management to senior executives.

Chapter 6: Phase II Findings: How Do You Sell Project Management to Senior Executives?

Chapter 6 presents the key findings from the comparative EFA on eight key models. The eight models included the General Selling Base Model, the Project Personnel Selling Model, the Consultant Selling Model, the Very Successful Selling Base Model, the Very Successful Project Personnel Model, the Very Successful Consultant Model, the Very Unsuccessful Selling Model, and the Senior Executive Model. The comparison among models identifies distinct differences between the models created from the very successful and very unsuccessful sellers, and also between the project personnel data and the consultant data.

What Do Very Successful Sellers Do?

Those reporting being very successful in selling project management to senior executives recognize the importance of context in setting and managing realistic expectations. These sellers tend to use arguments that highlight a variety of value statements about financial measures, staff growth, customer satisfaction, competition, and non-financial performance, and link them to issues/values of interest to senior executives.

The very successful sellers also use project management outcomes and practices as important sales arguments. Their arguments focus on project management as a senior executive decision, framing it in positive business language that speaks to solving problems. In terms of process, very successful sellers focus on explaining the fit between project management and the corporation or organization. Ultimately, very successful sellers pay attention to the quality of the relationship, and may be more adept at shifting arguments as the business context changes over time, thus creating lasting buyer-seller relations.

In general, successful sellers link project management to corporate strategies and position project management as a solution to problems. There are distinct differences between the approaches of successful project personnel and consultants. Unique to the very successful project personnel is their identification of realistic senior executive expectations as the most important contextual factor. Thus, they lead sales discussions with arguments related to "iron triangle" (time, cost, and scope) outcomes, framing them in executive language. However, they hone in on a smaller set of specific value statements about organizational development outcomes, rather than financial measures.

In contrast, the very successful consultants pay attention to the "accidental project manager" phenomenon and the organization's competitive situation. Consultants shape selling arguments around a variety of value statements, using statements crafted for the individual client and timing. They also use executive language in framing iron triangle arguments, while aligning project management goals with corporate goals and executive expectations. The consultants pay attention to the relationship and political nature of the sales process, recognizing that the arguments they use and the way they are framed are actually part of the entire sales process. In addition, very successful consultants often use value statements as processes to tie project management to an important corporate goal, rather than infer that project management will deliver such a benefit on its *own merits*. This strategy allows consultants to indirectly or directly tie the sale of project management to themselves or success of the project management implementation. In effect, this approach reduces the pressure to meet senior executive expectations of project management that may be set too high or not managed well.

What Do Unsuccessful Sellers Do?

A glaring difference between the successful and unsuccessful models relates to the prioritization and type of factors in the model. Unsuccessful sellers pay attention to making similar selling arguments, but fail to recognize the importance of the contextual issue and fail to use relation-based processes. They use an unrelated mix or "hodgepodge" of sales arguments, mostly containing executive language words in combination with dramatic emotional terms. The unsuccessful sellers use competitive arguments couched in emotional and dramatic terms that tend to decrease the seller's credibility. They focus more on shaping arguments around value statements that emphasize the quantitative benefit or effect on profits, market share, and competitive position. Ironically, these very arguments are likely to be the most difficult to justify or deliver, and are exactly the type of argument that the successful consultants, in particular, avoid.

What Are Senior Executives Looking For?

Senior executives report seeking business results, and want to achieve them through an emphasis on the iron triangle. However, they also report being open to a far wider array of value statements around project management then they are typically presented with. Senior executives are also more likely to pay attention to project management when someone with whom they have a relationship based on credibility and trust presents it.

Overall, these results suggest that senior executives are mainly interested in information that presents key aspects of project management as they relate to the business context of their organization, whether that means quantitative or qualitative results. They also want to hear about past successes, case studies, and any form of evidence to help them see the payoffs.

Chapter 7: Insights and Future Research Directions

Chapter 7 highlights the most important insights garnered over the course of the study, and puts forth practical and research-oriented recommendations.

In general, very successful project personnel and consultants place a different emphasis on, but commonly use, executive language, discuss the corporate fit, and present it as a value proposition when selling project management. In addition, it appears that some selling practices are unsuccessful. The very unsuccessful project personnel and consultants use many approaches that the very successful project personnel and consultants do not.

There does not appear to be one best sales strategy that should be applied across the board, because successful selling is sensitive to the instability of ever-changing client priorities and contexts, such as the global business climate. In essence, the approach that works for one seller may not work for another. As well, there are many different ways that salespeople themselves influence and shape the way project management is sold.

While there do not appear to be any "silver bullets," or universal truths, to successfully selling project management to senior executives, there are guidelines that effective salespeople can employ to bring project management to the attention of senior executives. We recommend adopting a three-pronged approach. First, identify what triggers the executive's interest in issues. Second, develop a portfolio of responses for the various types of executive triggers. Finally, back up each response with evidence relevant to the organization and the executive you are working with. In addition, we provide insights from research on selling strategic issues to senior executives. These guidelines help contextualize the "sales project" and provide approaches for developing and framing arguments and implementing a "sales process" within a particular organization.

This chapter concludes with recommendations for future researchers on the required follow-up to this study.

CHAPTER 1

Study Background

Organizational theory has much to contribute to the development of project management research. In particular, two important organizational concepts are "wicked problems" (Lyles 1987) and "knowing-doing gaps" (Pfeffer and Sutton 2000). The term wicked problem applies to disconcerting issues that are challenging, frustrating, and difficult to pin down and solve. The knowing-doing gap, as described by Pfeffer and Sutton (2000), refers to having the knowledge of what needs to be done, but frequently failing to act or behaving inconsistently with that knowledge. The presence of a knowing-doing gap at the highest levels of organizational management can be seen when senior executives successfully explain what their company needs to do strategically, but the company does not actually implement these strategic plans.

Those selling project management to senior executives face wicked problems in bringing project management onto senior executives' radar screens with the hopes that it will be valued, invested in, and used. Sellers also run into knowing-doing gaps in the implementation of project management in organizations today. One particularly wide gap is evident in terms of our understanding that senior executive support and involvement is critical to the success of most projects and our inability to interest senior executives in project management.

The presence of wicked problems and knowing-doing gaps complicates efforts to sell project management to senior executives. The bottom line is that the advantage in investing in project management goes to companies that know how, and commit, to use the knowledge they have, instead of to firms that have the best knowledge but do not act on it. Thus, if organizations are to reap the strategic benefits of project management that many believe are possible, it is fundamentally important that these problems are solved and these gaps in senior executives' interest in project management are bridged.

In 1998, project management practitioners, through the Project Management Institute (PMI®), identified a gap between perceived interest in project management at the senior executive level and the investment in project management. The practitioners also identified a strong interest in how to interest senior executives in project management. Consequently, PMI issued an international request for research proposals on "Best Practices for Communicating the Benefits of Project Management to Senior Executives." This report documents the research project that was selected for support as a result of the PMI proposal process. This project studied why it was difficult to sell project management to senior executives and how project management is successfully sold to them. This project was partially funded by PMI, with significant contributions from Athabasca University, The University of Calgary, IBM Canada, Computers in Information Processing Society Canada, ESI-International, PMI Southern Alberta Chapter, and CIO Canada.

The remainder of this chapter describes the research objectives, key definitions, research questions, scope limitations, the research team structure and management process, timing and deliverables, and structure of this book.

Research Objectives

The primary objective of this study was to better understand the process of how project personnel and consultants increase senior executive interest in project management. Specifically, the research team set out to:

- Identify the main arguments put forth to sell (promote) project management to senior executives, or in other words, bring project management to their attention.
- Articulate the effective strategies used to sell project management to senior executives.

The research investigation was divided into two phases. In Phase I, the objective was to understand why the very people who best understood project management within organizations (i.e., project managers) seem to have the hardest time selling it to their senior executives, as compared to external consultants and other project management experts. We believed that unraveling this paradox would help identify strategies and practices essential in creating awareness of the benefits of project management, such that it would be easier to become successful at selling project management to senior executives.

In Phase II, the objective was to identify the specific "best practices" related to the process, arguments, and context of successfully selling project management to senior executives. To accomplish this objective we needed to be able to ensure that the findings of Phase I interpretations, on why selling project management to senior executives was difficult, be integrated in Phase II. Then we needed to explore the status of project management practice in today's organizations to see what kind of context or milieu faces those selling project management. Finally, we needed to identify issues, approaches, and compelling arguments used in selling project management to senior executives. In other words, we needed to understand the process, arguments, and context of the larger selling concept.

By exploring situations where project management has been successfully or unsuccessfully implemented in organizations, this research sought to find the key reasons why selling was successful in some cases and not in others.

Key Definitions

For this study, "project management" is operationally defined as the disciplines, methodologies, processes, and standards applied to managing projects in the workplace. The concept of "selling" is defined as promoting and advocating project management to senior executives in an organized manner to bring it to their attention. The term "project personnel" includes all organizational personnel involved in project management. This could include team leaders and project control officers up to, and including, program directors. Most of the project personnel are at the project manager or program director level. The term "consultants" refers to individuals involved in selling project management services and tools to organizations (at times as part of selling products to clients, i.e., information technology systems). For the purposes of this study, "senior executives" are defined as individuals at the vice president level or higher, that sponsor projects in their organizations.

In this study, we use the word "seller" to describe those project personnel or consultants who bring the discipline to the attention of senior executives. We use the word "buyer" to mean the group of senior executives in a position to make organizational decisions around the investment in project management.

Research Questions

A practical management question initiated this study, "What are the best practices in communicating the value of project management to senior executives?" However, answering this question requires peeling off many layers of issues to get to the core. Before trying to answer the original question, we first needed to understand the underlying issues around selling project management to senior executives. As well, we needed to understand the process, arguments, and context involved in the entire selling milieu. As a start, the management question must be broken into specific research questions, to allow for the depth of understanding required to conduct a meaningful investigation. The purpose in doing so relates to the need to discover underlying concepts that can then be operationalized (defined) and measured. As introduced previously, the two primary research questions are:

- Why is it difficult to sell project management to senior executives?
- How do you successfully sell project management to senior executives?

Within each primary research question, a host of sub-questions surfaced during the course of the literature review and primary analysis of pilot data. The set of sub-questions grew as the investigation proceeded, generating more pieces of the selling puzzle and making connections between existing beliefs about selling project management to senior executives. Our job became one of a tactician, to skillfully interweave the pieces of the puzzle, as well as strategist, to clearly see the big picture and ensure the key parts of the puzzle received the most in-depth attention. To address the issue of why it is difficult to sell project management to senior executives we needed to explore general (*) and specific (**) sub-questions, as follows:

- How are selling, marketing, and project management related?*

- What are senior executives looking for in managing projects?*

- How do sellers and buyers of project management interact?*

- Why is it important to align the values of sellers and buyers in the sales process?*

- How is project management typically sold in organizations?**

- What triggers senior executive interest in project management?**

- What are the barriers to selling project management?**

Selling of any product or service does not occur in a vacuum. Thus, good research recognizes the need to clearly understand the larger content in which events take place, to lay a foundation to continue investigations into how the selling processes evolves as circumstances change. To begin, we placed a stake in the ground and examined the current context of selling.

Research Approach

This section provides a brief overview of the research approach used in conducting this research project. The actual steps in the research approach for each phase are described in Chapter 3.

Given the magnitude of questions and the types of answers needed to fully understand them, the study needed to balance rigor and relevance. In short, both qualitative (in depth, rich meanings from small amounts of data) and quantitative (succinct, more broad meaning from larger quantities of data research) approaches were employed. In many studies, statistics are manipulated skillfully to tell the story of the research findings. To ensure the quality of our story, statistical techniques were considered a means to an end to help make sense of the data, not provide interpretations beyond the strength of the numbers. Tying the level of analysis to the data collection instrument measurement level, sample size, and purpose in answering the research questions helped to keep the focus on what the data itself was saying.

To achieve a suitable balance, we conducted the research in two phases. Phase I consisted of a literature review of the project management, marketing, and organizational theory bodies of knowledge to develop a general framework for understanding the issues related to selling project management to senior executives (see Chapter 2). The initial wide angle of the literature review was narrowed down by identifying key concepts of interest to the study that essentially guided the development of the qualitatively focused interview questions. As a spin off, this phase also enabled us to draw in important literature for review that relates to selling issues, as discussed by prominent researchers outside of the field of project management (Dutton et al. 2000; Dutton and Ashford 1993; Dutton and Webster 1988).

Personal interviews with three types of subjects (N = 25) served as the source of data for the qualitative analysis. These groups represented experienced practitioners familiar with selling and purchasing project management—internal project personnel, project management consultants/experts, and senior executives with project management purchasing power. At least two of us conducted each interview to ensure consistency in data collection.

A grounded theory analytic approach helped us identify trends or themes related to successful and unsuccessful sales strategies. Unlike conventional research approaches, the analysis takes place during, as well as after, the data collection. For example, as the interviews progressed, the interviewers noted the emergence of particular issues, themes, and points. Particular attention was paid to the similarities and differences in how the groups, as a whole, understood project management and its benefits. The reoccurrence of key issues, themes, and trends signaled the presence of core concepts related to the research question. (See Chapter 4 for the results of this phase.)

Due to the exploratory intent of the first phase, the limited sample provided a rich data set, rather than one that claims to be statistically generalizable to the greater population. With so many unaddressed questions about the topic of study, Phase I provided the direction for shaping the data collection for Phase II.

Armed with the knowledge from Phase 1, Phase II addressed the question, "How do you successfully sell project management to senior executives?" The foundation of the data collection instrument (questionnaire survey) lies in conclusions coming from confirmation of, or challenges to, results initially examined and interpretations of concepts generated from the Phase I analysis, literature review findings, discussions with experts in the field, and examination of previous questionnaires on similar topics. Ultimately the instrument contained sixty-two questions. The instrument was validated in a pilot study of project management experts and practitioners.

Because of the lack of research rigor in the relatively young body of project management research, much time and energy were needed to design and pre-test suitable data collection instruments. As well, policies and regulations for obtaining permission for electronic data collection on individual and organizational levels necessitated that the scope be limited to a two-phase approach. This study serves as both an exploratory effort, as well as one that provides the profession with a methodologically solid foundation to conduct further research into the area.

A professional survey company used the Internet to enable the collection of data from suitable participants worldwide. Of these 3,093 respondents that accessed the survey, the useable sample totaled 1,868 participants, for a response rate of 5.3 percent overall. The survey accuracy rate of +/- 2.27 percent (19 times out of 20) means that the questionnaire provided data that is statistically valid, not occurring by chance. The integrity of the size of the dataset, combined with careful comparison of underlying demographics of the sample and respondents, allows for generalizability of the findings.

Scope Limitations

The scope of this study is limited to addressing the research questions for Phases I and II, to meet the stated research objectives. To adequately address these questions, review of the literature covered a breath of topic areas about selling, project management, project success, marketing, organizational theory, and so on, in order to generate a well-rounded picture of the research. Some of the more technical aspects of these literatures were reviewed, but not included in the literature review for this report, to keep the focus on selling as a process within project management. The core of the literature review served as a base for the framework we developed to drill down to the key concepts involved in effective selling strategies.

Another scope limitation relates to the choices made in analyzing the wealth of data we collected in Phase II. The main dataset included information on the state of project management issues (project management practices, project outcomes, project management preparation, executive attention) in selling project management to senior executives (value of project management, successful arguments, successful approaches), and project manager preparation (demand for education, experience level, level of education). Since this information goes far beyond PMI's requirements for this project, the data collected on subtopics outside the scope of the primary research questions will be the subject of future research projects.

This report focuses more on our interpretation of the findings, instead of explaining the methodology or describing statistical procedures. We assume that readers have a basic understanding of statistics. The report contains some key statistical definitions that are less common so readers can follow what was done. Those interested in further information on methodology and statistical analysis techniques are referred to the following sources or are welcome to contact us (Bagozzi 1984; Barry 1998; Bickman and Rog 1998; Bryman 2000; Cresswell 1996; Dahlen 1998; Flick 1998; Gray and Guppy 1999; Hair et al. 1998; Hill 1998; Marcolin 2001; Mason 1998; Maxwell 1996; McLaughlin 1999).

Team Structure and Management Process

Our core project team involved the three researchers listed below, as well as Ms. Pamela Buckle, who assisted the researchers in Phase I. This section briefly outlines our team structure and the project management processes we used to collect data and complete this research report.

Dr. Janice Thomas, Principal Investigator
Program Director and Online Executive MBA in Project Management
Centre for Innovative Management
Athabasca University
Adjunct Professor, Project Management Specialization
University of Calgary
Email: JaniceT@Athabascau.ca
Phone: 403-949-4965
Website: http://www.athabascau.ca/mba

Dr. Connie Delisle, Research Associate
Academic Coach and Online Course Developer
Center for Innovative Management
Athabasca University
Email: Connie_Delisle@mba.athabascau.ca

Kam Jugdev, Research Associate
PhD Student, University of Calgary
Academic Coach and Online Course Developer
Center for Innovative Management
Athabasca University
Email: kjugdev@shaw.ca

Pamela Buckle, Research Assistant (Involved in Phase 1)
Teaching Assistant
Faculty of Management
University of Calgary
Email: pmbuckle@shaw.ca

From a communications perspective, the team completed monthly project status reports for the PMI Research Program Manager and the liaison to the PMI Research Program Member Advisory Group (RMAG). Dr. Thomas regularly discussed the project with the RMAG representative and met with both the PMI Research Program Manager and RMAG on three occasions over the course of the two-year project. As a virtual team, the core project members held weekly conference calls that were documented. They used a variety of communication techniques to share project information including shareware, email, and so on. They also met every few months face-to-face for replanning, or for group discussion of research progress and findings. The leadership tended to shift with the expertise of the team, producing a climate to openly discuss the project.

Timing and Deliverables

Phase I of the project began in November 1999 and was completed in September 2000. Deliverables of the first phase included learning about why it is difficult to sell project management to senior executives, and completion of a series of public communications. The public communications included:

- A conference paper and presentation at the *PMI Research Conference 2000* in Paris, France (Thomas et al. 2000a)

- A conference paper and presentation at the *PMI 2000 Seminars and Symposium* in Houston, Texas USA in September 2000 (Thomas et al. 2000b)

- A journal article in *PM Network*® (Thomas et al. 2001a)

- A journal article in the *Project Management Journal*® (Thomas et al. 2001c) (submitted and accepted).

A high level Gantt chart for Phase I was prepared and is illustrated in Table 1.1.

Phase II began in October 2000 and was largely completed by December 2001. Data was collected in March 2001. Major deliverables for this phase included learning about best practices for selling project management to senior executives to

Table 1.1. Phase I Project Gantt Chart

ID	Task Name	Duration	Start	Finish
1	**PHASE 1**	**300 days**	**Aug 16**	**Oct 3**
2	**Structure, research and write papers**	**147 days**	**Nov 5**	**May 26**
3	Conduct literature search	16 days	Nov 5	Nov 26
4	Complete literature review	0 days	Nov 26	Nov 26
5	Organize project, budget, staffing	20 days	Nov 15	Dec 10
6	Complete budget and staffing	0 days	Dec 10	Dec 10
7	Develop survey instruments	25 days	Nov 22	Dec 24
8	Complete survey instrument	0 days	Feb 11	Feb 11
9	Collect data	50 days	Feb 14	Apr 21
10	Complete data collection	15 days	Apr 24	May 12
11	Complete focus group sessions	0 days	May 12	May 12
12	Conduct analysis and synthesis	10 days	May 15	May 26
13	Complete analysis and papers	0 days	May 26	May 26
14	**Conference Presentations/Paper revisions**	**300 days**	**Aug 16**	**Oct 3**
15	Prepare foils for Paris, Houston conf.	5 days	Aug 16	Aug 20
16	Present at PMI (Paris)	0 days	Jun 23	Jun 23
17	Prepare *PM Network* paper for submission	15 days	Sep 13	Oct 3
18	**Status reports**	**1 day**	**Mar 30**	**Mar 30**
19	Submit status reports to funders	1 day	Mar 30	Mar 30
20	**COMPLETE PHASE 1**	0 days	Nov 10	Nov 10

find out how to sell project management to senior executives, and completion of a series of public communications. The public communications included:

- A conference paper and presentation at the *PMI 2001 Seminars and Symposium* in Nashville, Tennessee USA in November 2001 (Thomas et al. 2001b)

- A conference paper and presentation at the *PMI Research Conference 2002* in Seattle, Washington USA in July 2002 (Thomas, Delisle, and Jugdev 2002a)

- This research report (Thomas, Delisle, and Jugdev 2002b).

A high level Gantt chart for Phase II was prepared and is illustrated in Table 1.2.

The project met the budget constraints and most of the major milestones, but was slightly late in delivery of the final report. Most importantly, the project met our own and the client's expectations.

Report Structure

The report contains seven chapters that tell the story of this research study, processes, and outcomes. This first chapter provides an introduction to the topic of study, the research purpose and scope, research objectives, research questions, limitations, and the management of this research project. The remaining chapters provide more details on each of the parts of the research study.

- Chapter 2: Theoretical Foundation
- Chapter 3: Study Methodology

Table 1.2. Phase II Project Gantt Chart

ID		Task Name	Duration	Start	Finish
1		**PHASE 2**	**646 days**	**Aug 16**	**Jan 30**
2		**Conferences fall 2000**	**288 days**	**Aug 16**	**Sep 15**
3		Prepare for PMI Houston conference	3.25 days	Aug 16	Aug 19
4		Present at PMI Houston - practitioner	6 days	Sep 9	Sep 15
5		**Online survey instrument**	**142.5 days**	**Sep 1**	**Mar 16**
6		Develop Delphi and Web instruments	105 days	Sep 1	Jan 24
7		Complete Delphi and Web instruments	0 days	Jan 24	Jan 24
8		Conduct pilot tests	37.5 days	Jan 25	Mar 16
9		Complete pilot tests	0 days	Mar 16	Mar 16
10		**Data collection**	**225 days**	**Mar 16**	**Jan 23**
11		Collect data	150 days	Mar 16	Oct 10
12		Complete data collection	0 days	Oct 10	Oct 10
13		Conduct focus group sessions	75 days	Oct 10	Jan 23
14		**Data analysis and writing**	**154 days**	**Jan 23**	**Aug 27**
15		Conduct analysis	69 days	Jan 23	Apr 30
16		Complete analysis and synthesis	0 days	Apr 30	Apr 30
17		Draft paper(s)	40 days	Apr 30	Jun 25
18		Write manuscript	45 days	Jun 25	Aug 27
19		**Submit monthly status reports to PMI**	**504 days**	**Feb 29**	**Jan 30**
20		**COMPLETE PHASE 2**	0 days	Nov 30	Nov 30

- Chapter 4: Findings from Phase I: Why Is it Difficult to Sell Project Management to Senior Executives?

- Chapter 5: Findings from Phase II: Demographics and Practices

- Chapter 6: Findings from Phase II: How Do You Sell Project Management to Senior Executives?

- Chapter 7: Insights and Future Research Directions

Our investment in this report is evident, in part, in the length. Rather than try to summarize our findings in the last chapter, each chapter concludes with a brief summary. Chapter 7 attempts to highlight the most significant and practical research findings and contributions.

Support material for this study is in the appendices and reference sections.

CHAPTER 2

Theoretical Foundation

This chapter provides a brief overview of the challenges to building a theoretical foundation for this study, and explains the framework used to investigate what senior executives want, what the benefits of project management are, and how it is currently being sold and understood.

Project management is a relatively new discipline in the scope of academic fields of study. As well, project management is a cross-functional area, whose roots initially sprang from management and engineering practice, coming only recently to research inquiry. As such, project management has a strong practice-based foundation, but a very underdeveloped empirical base, and an even weaker theoretical presence. The opening of what Urli and Urli (2000) refer to as a "decentralization" of project management knowledge, has occurred by borrowing from established disciplines (Chalmers 1999; Delisle 2001; DiMaggio 1995; Reynolds 1971; Shaw and Gaines 1995; Sutton and Staw 1995; Thomas 2000; Urli and Urli 2000; Weick 1995). This borrowing has forced the discipline to quickly gather resources and engage researchers who will broaden and expand the depth of knowledge about pressing issues in project management that underlay "wicked problems." Thus, people- or socially-focused research is starting to play an increasingly important role in a discipline originally most interested in getting the job done with the right technical tools and techniques.

This project began at a point in time marked by a fertile climate of possibility, albeit one riddled with many unanswered questions about basic project management knowledge. Thomas (2000) identifies that professionals in project management do not seem to share a common understanding of what project management is, thus, making it difficult to build a cohesive, contemporary knowledge base grounded in theory.

The formation of any major body of knowledge begins with a profession simply describing problems faced by managers, to eventually reveal phenomena, serving as the first step in an iterative process of theory building (Christensen and Sundahl 1999). A rich knowledge base results from practitioners and researchers questioning, challenging, and eventually understanding key concepts, issues, processes, strategies, and practices, e.g., making sense in the context of project management.

The next step in theory building is to take this knowledge and begin to classify it into similar categories as a way of high-level organizing to allow for generalizing of knowledge (Christensen and Sundahl 1999). At this point, researchers have the foundation on which to begin to develop theories that describe, and eventually explain, how a phenomenon within this body of knowledge behaves. Good theories, once tested, reveal paradoxes or unpredicted events (Sutton and Staw 1995). By feeding findings and interpretations back into the first step, and cycling through the process, theory, after much iteration, starts to describe, or even explain, a paradigm or standard. Finally, these standards form the foundations of a true "profession" (Christensen and Sundahl 1999).

Many issues of concern that underlay this research investigation have not been studied empirically in the project management realm. As well, the Project Management Institute (PMI®) and others are just in the early stages of investigating potentially viable project classification systems. Because theory building, project classification, and the development of project management as a profession appear inextricably meshed, answering how to sell project management is somewhat like hitting a moving target.

Thus, the small, but important, body of practical knowledge and conceptual (opinion and case reports) type of research served as the study's initial foundation. We sought to broaden this base by exploring the project management, marketing, and organizational literature. In particular, research in the areas of relationship marketing and developing trust and credibility are important foundations for this work. Finally, issues of strategic issue management (Dutton and Ashford 1993; Dutton et al. 1997; 2001) and organizational "sense making" (summarized in Weick 1995) are critical to building successful arguments and developing accepted processes. This literature review provided a broad base and provided the richness and depth of information necessary in beginning to investigate the issues around selling project management to senior executives.

The following sections provide an introduction to the areas of the project management, marketing, and organizational theory literature examined in the study. Each section provides several citations to point interested readers towards important further readings. A full bibliographical reference is included at the end of this book.

Project Management Literature

Project management is a growing discipline practiced in challenging, competitive marketplaces. It is considered by many "one of a few critically enabling strategies for strengthening a competitive marketplace posture" (Bounds 1998, 41). The issue of selling project management to senior executives is a significant part of understanding successful project management because it involves senior management support, both financially and in managerial terms. Achieving support for the discipline enables firms to improve their competitive advantage (Belassi and Tukel 1996; Pinto and Slevin 1987; Shenhar, Levy, and Dvir 1997).

Thus, we examine five critical areas of project management literature, including the practical literature on selling project management, the research literature on project success, the value of project management, the role of sense making in successful project management, and project management practices.

Practical Literature on Selling Project Management

Over the last ten years, the topic of selling project management has generated interest within the PMI community, as evidenced by papers presented at *PMI Seminars and Symposium* (Block 1991; 1992). Resulting publications focus on describing the value of project management to senior executives to gain their support and commitment for the project and related funding. Kerzner discusses selling project management to senior management using a two-step approach. First, the functional managers need to identify the need for it and then, executives need to be sold on the concept. Kerzner suggests that external consultants, rather than internal staff, most effectively sell to executives, as consultants tend to be viewed as being more impartial (Kerzner 2001).

Project Success

Worldwide, project management is gaining acceptance in many industry sectors. Increasingly, companies espouse project management as an important competency. On one hand, the literature reviewed for this book discusses a growing interest in the use of elements of project management in virtually every segment of every industry. On the other hand, over 30 percent of projects end up being cancelled in midstream, and over half of information technology (IT) projects run as high as 190 percent over budget and 220 percent over the original time estimate (KPMG 1997; Standish 1996; 2001). Morris and Hough (1987) found similar results in engineering construction projects.

Much of this bad news seems to derive from confusion around the metrics used and the measures considered important. Traditionally, the "iron triangle" measures of budget, schedule, and scope take predominance in success/outcome studies. Toney and Powers' (1997) research finds that project teams most commonly use the success outcome measurements, "on budget" (58 percent), "on time" (81 percent), and "quality" (69 percent), but only 19 percent of respondents measure customer satisfaction and fewer mention market success (15 percent). On the other hand, Delisle (2001) finds that respondents (N = 50) are only successful 21 percent of the time in actually "meeting the budget" and 23 percent of the time in "meeting the schedule." Earlier empirical research by Shenhar, Levy, and Dvir (1997) and more recently Delisle

(2001), finds exactly the same thing—that "budget and schedule" form a distinct factor to help explain project success. However, both Shenhar, Levy, and Dvir (1997) and Delisle (2001) find similar results in that the "budget and schedule" factor accounted for only 10 percent of the variance or ability to explain the success of a project. Furthermore, Delisle's (2001) results show that an "effectiveness factor" comprised of "solving the business problem, fulfilling customers needs, product or service being used by customer, satisfying the customer, and generating a large market share" accounts for just over 40 percent of the ability to explain the variance of project success. In short, evidence points to a wide knowing-doing gap, which brings awareness to the need to reconsider the range of criteria currently relied on to determine the status of project outcomes.

Furthermore, managing expectations also plays a key role in understanding project success. Directly to the point, Lim and Mohamed (1999) discuss the need to link what executives should pay attention to (success indicators) with what they are actually tracking to meet the bottom line (success criteria). Adding to this, Delisle (2001) reports that an astounding *20 percent* of participants report not taking the time up front in the planning phase to identify success indicators *or* success criteria.

Despite the research evidence, literature reports of the high failure rate of projects, and advocacy of project management by practitioners, long-term investment in project management is difficult to attain and is seriously needed. Knowing how to get around the tough sell at the senior executive level is certainly necessary in sparking their interest to make an investment. According to KPMG's (1997) survey of over 1,400 organizations, the lack of top management commitment is a key factor in failed projects. The independent research from the Standish Group (1996; 2001) also supports this conclusion. Clearly, project failure, the role of project management, and senior executive level support are connected, and each needs to be addressed.

Unfortunately, industry has come to depend on and demand consistency in market-based research that focuses on finding the one "right" list of critical criteria that is vital to the delivery of successful projects (Delisle 2001). Rockhart's original study of success factors suggests that a core group of success factors works within a specific process to influence project delivery, but he also makes it clear that success factors vary by project and industry (Rockhart and Short 1991). Although Rockhart's study appears as foundational to the body of knowledge on success, advancements need to be made to reduce the emphasis on ranking elements or individual success criteria. Much can be gained by examining what combination of success criteria is most capable of predicting project success at key points along the project life cycle, and understanding how and why this influences the overall project and product outcome.

Overall, it is highly conceivable that perceptions of past experiences with project failures influence senior executives' buying behavior for future project management services. Traditional perceptions are that marketing and sales staff "oversell" project management services, and then the delivery team faces challenges and wicked problems in meeting heightened senior management expectations. Managing expectations is often mentioned as critical to success in project management and project outcomes, and it relates to the role that marketing and sales perform (Pinto and Covin 1989; Pinto and Mantel 1990; Pinto and Prescott 1990; Pinto and Slevin 1987; 1988a; 1988b; 1989). Thus, selling of services involves a balance of knowing what to expect, taking the time to set expectations, and managing "doing something about" expectations throughout the sales cycle, as well as the project life cycle (ABT 2000). Even more so in a globally competitive business environment, the project life cycle and the sales cycle are interlinked, and should not be viewed, or treated, as mutually exclusive.

Value of Project Management

Considering the preceding discussion of project success, it stands to reason that current literature on the valuation of project management commonly reports that measured efficiency terms (time, cost, and scope) and financial terms are generally limited to the project, as opposed to broader valuation practices that extend to the organization (Belassi and Tukel 1996; Clarke 1999; Kerzner 1987; Munns and Bjeirmi 1996; Shenhar, Levy, and Dvir 1997). The literature review supports the premise that project management's value is generally perceived to be at the operational level, and that it is still mostly studied and treated as a tactical concept. The marketing literature we review next shows that senior executives generally focus on corporate issues and those related to business strategy and results (Barney 2001; Dutton et al. 2000). This gap is also part of the conundrum within project management that impacts the sale of project management. How do sellers get senior executives on the supportive side of project management when the prevailing belief is that it is a tactical tool/technique of little or no importance at the strategic level?

Practitioners believe they need generalizable, quantitative evidence to show to senior executives to even attempt to make a value argument really work, and to work around the engrained beliefs and negative perceptions that can hamper the sale of project management. However, research into quantitatively demonstrating the economic value is scarce. PMI has sponsored seminal work conducted by Ibbs and his team (1997; 1998; 2000) that has noted the challenges inherent in gathering highly sensitive financial information from competing companies. They also note, "Many organizations are uncertain, perplexed, and even misdirected about the status of current applications of project management. Moreover, the financial investment in project management tools, practices, and processes is often seen as quite difficult to justify" (Ibbs and Kwak 2000, 32.) In their most current study on assessing project management maturity in thirty-eight firms, Ibbs and Kwak found that "many companies did not see the true value in this research, or they were reluctant to share the details of their project management practices" (Ibbs and Kwak 2000, 36). Thus, experience has shown that statistically generalizable quantitative dollar costs and benefits associated with project management are extremely difficult, if not impossible, to measure, and furthermore, research suggests that they are not adequate to fully communicate the intangible and future benefit type of value of project management.

The foregoing review of the status of our understanding of project management value provides a foundation from which to study the value statements in use in project management selling efforts. In particular, this study must explore the value statements sellers are using to interest senior executives in project management. In addition, it is important to determine the value senior executives are in fact interested in.

Understandings of Project Management

Part of developing a relationship with customers involves understanding and conveying the merits of project management to them. The practical benefits, as paraphrased by Dinsmore (1996) and McElroy (1996), seem simple and obvious.

- Providing a coordinated and aligned interface between partners and stakeholders at the project and organization level.

- Positioning an organization in a strong global orientation by accelerating implementation of corporate strategies.

- Managing extensive political pressure to deliver on unrealistic time frames.

- Developing operational and performance standards to ensure quality, control spending, and reduce time to market.

- Providing structure and practical methods for planning complex, and often emergent, customer needs.

- Prioritizing and selecting rationale, because not all projects are equally value adding.

However, research finds that project management concepts are not well understood and the value of project management is not a shared concept (Thomas 2000; Tjaeder 1999). This research shows that different groups on the same project understood and valued typical concepts differently. These gaps in sense making are an integral part of serious communication and expectation failures. Differences may lie in the interpretation of even simple ways of conveying the benefits of project management, along with ideas about what is actually done in planning a project, for example.

Although project management is perceived to have value towards improving operational efficiency and contributing to a firm's competitive advantage, the perceptions of its organizational benefits are not always aligned among the senior executives who may buy or invest in the services, the practitioners who apply the discipline, and the consultants who are involved in selling it. Senior executives focus on business goals, results, and outcomes from projects, while practitioners and consultants tend to focus on the tactics of tools and techniques to showcase the "latest and greatest" project management advancements. Research suggests there are substantial language barriers among these groups in project management, and there exists considerable difficulty in developing a shared understanding and appreciation of project management (Thomas 2000). These sense making gaps could be a serious barrier to selling project management to senior executives, clearly calling for further examination.

Project Management Practices

Contributing to these varying understandings and valuations, is the fact that there is very little commonality of practice of project management across organizations. Different organizations implement different aspects of the tools and techniques, as well as methodologies, and label it all "project management."

Recognition of this variability is seen in the extensive efforts during the 1990s to develop and market project management maturity models (PMM)(AIPM 2000; APM 2001; CCTA 2000; Dinsmore 1998; ESI-International 2001; Hartman and Skulmoski 1998; IPMA 2000; Lubianiker and Schwartz 2001; Schlichter 1999). In addition, efforts are underway to develop global project management competency standards (Crawford 1998; Turner and Crawford 1994).

Project management maturity models are not presently theory based, but they do assess processes, practices, and outcomes related to the effective use of the discipline. Mostly, PMMs can help organizations gain a better feel for how advanced or mature they are in the use of project management. Most of the models involve five linear stages of practice maturity: Level 1(initial), Level 2 (repeatable), Level 3 (defined), Level 4 (managed), and Level 5 (optimized). The PMMs are mostly based on the Software Engineering Institute's Capability Maturity Models (CMM) (SEI 2001). At the moment, there are a number of PMMs in existence and use, although global support and exclusive use by any one industry type or professional body for a particular model has not materialized.

The reasons behind efforts to develop and use a PMM might speak to the perceived need to increase the credibility and measurability of project management practices and benefits. This standardization, and related trend with certification practices, appears to be an argument that some organizations and/or senior executives may be willing to accept as part of their investment in project management. Part of the problem may be in the ambiguity of the cause and effect relationship—are executives unwilling to invest because a model has not yet achieved global recognition to be the accepted standard, or has a model not yet achieved global recognition because of lack of investment? Furthermore, the maturity models are operationally focused on project or divisional practices, adding to the perceived value of project management being tied to the tactical level. Since senior executives focus more on corporate directions, these models have not convinced senior executives of their strategic value. Furthermore, many resist these models, as they do not fully appreciate the benefits relative to the effort in terms of documentation and procedural requirements to move from one level to the next (Lubianiker and Schwartz 2001). As a result, PMMs have merit in developing standardized practices, but investment at the senior executive level remains a difficult sell. Future research will need to pay attention to PMM levels and their link to perceptions of value.

Marketing Literature

At its core, marketing literature documents how successful sellers present the service or product in a practical manner that speaks to the issues of the purchaser. The literature provides basic tenets of marketing that include: developing rapport, meeting with the decision-makers, and having credibility (Gardner and Bistritz 1998; Gardner, Bistritz, and Klompmaker 1996; Heinrichs 2000; King 1994; 1996; Marchetti 1997; OnTarget 1999; Price 1999; Weitz and Bradford 1999). Prior to this research, few have related these concepts specifically to project management. This section provides brief introductions to each of the relevant marketing literatures we explored as a foundation for this study, including literature on services marketing, seller credibility, branding, sales tactics, and aligning buying and selling values.

Services Marketing

Early in our investigation of the marketing literature, we decided that project management has more of the characteristics of a service than a product. Thus, we focused on the marketing issues related to services marketing. Some researchers view selling products and services as similar. Ward, Light, and Goldstine, and other researchers, view selling on a continuum with "product selling," differing from "services selling" (Bistritz, Gardner, and Klompmaker 1998; Bistritz et al. 1999; EIU 1999; Gardner and Bistritz 1998; Ward, Light, and Goldstine 1999). Competitors can more readily copy products, but services are harder to mimic. Services are also more dependent on a firm's culture, values, and practices and involve staff training and attitudes (Ward, Light, and Goldstine 1999). In general, the biggest difference is in the importance of relationships in services selling.

This literature helped us to understand some of the issues around selling project management. Selling project management as a product (a one-time investment) requires efficiency arguments and significant hard cost benefits to compete with all the other possible uses of these funds. However, recognition that "on time and on budget" success criteria have limited ability to explain project success, and quantitative arguments are generally tied to the tactical value of project management, sellers may need to consider relationship selling, based on the business or strategic value of project management. A foundation value such as efficiency appears necessary in developing the type of selling relationship so that the project services or solutions offered are aligned with the organization's business directions and its efforts to make good on the promise of value to customers.

Exploring the nature of the relationship and how it is built will be an important part of this research.

Seller Credibility

Trust and credibility appear to be critical to building a lasting sales relationship. Considerable marketing literature on selling services, and management literature on presenting issues to management, discusses how important it is for sellers to be perceived as credible (Bistritz et al. 1999; Block 1991; 1992; Dutton et al. 2000; Dutton and Ashford 1993; Dutton and Webster 1988; Gardner and Bistritz 1998; Gardner, Bistritz, and Klompmaker 1996).

Gardner, Bistritz, and Klompmaker (1996) researched key factors that help salespeople develop trust and credibility with senior executives. They report that the most effective ways of establishing trust and credibility with senior executives are to marshal resources from their own organization and understand the customer's goals/objectives, as well as being responsive to requests. They conclude, "the worst impression a salesperson can leave is wasted time" (Gardner, Bistritz, and Klompmaker 1996, 7). The relevance of this research is three-fold. First, it takes a unique research approach by interviewing senior executives, instead of simply examining buying/selling practices from just the salespeople's perspective. Second, it emphasizes how critical the relationship (e.g., trust and credibility) is in selling services. Third, it affirms that selling services involves strong soft skills on the part of the marketing/sales staff.

Since selling services does not end once the sale has been made, the project management team must continue to demonstrate strong interpersonal skills to ensure the success of the project sold. In terms of long-term relationship building at the senior executive level, sellers have to also consider the success an organization actually experiences once project management has been sold and implemented, which in turn has serious implications for seller credibility.

Branding

A brand is a distinctive identity that differentiates a promise of value associated with a product service (Ward, Light, and Goldstine 1999). Branding helps establish common value statements in the minds of both buyers and sellers. Ward, Light, and Goldstine (1999) suggest that branding is an effective method of simplifying how the promise of value is communicated to the purchaser. In turn, brand management is a means of embodying the value of products and services, through which an organization may create a strong relationship with its customer (Ward, Light, and Goldstine 1999). Macdonald and Sharp (1996) indicate that just being a known brand can dramatically affect their evaluation. This article is important because it points out how brand awareness can add value by placing the brand in the consumer's mind; acting as a barrier to entry of unestablished brands; communicating the competency of the services' organization; and providing leverage in the distribution channels where buyers are unsure. Thus, how and if project management can be branded is an issue of interest in evaluating how to sell project management to senior executives.

Effectively, organizations such as PMI have already established a brand or trusted source of project management knowledge and training. Thus, branding can become a powerful part of selling that hinges on trust and credibility. This, in turn, may tie into the equation needed to fully communicate the value of project management, and make re-entry for future sales less difficult.

Sales Tactics

Selling is a skill that develops over time and with practice. Over the past thirty years, there has been a noticeable shift in the three levels of sales proficiency. These levels include, tactical (sell products); strategic (work with the customer to find the right solution to business problems); and competitive (work with the customer to develop the business relationship that helps the customer achieve their business objectives). Gardner, Bistritz, and Klompmaker (1996) find that senior executives do not have a lot of time for tactical approaches.

Since current service selling benefits are believed to lie in using a competitive approach, the challenge for selling project management services will be in identifying, articulating, and achieving deliverables that are directly linked to corporate and business objectives. This goal is stated as a challenge and a knowing-doing gap, because companies purport to deliver on this basis of value, but project failure rates indicate otherwise.

Aligning Buying and Selling Values

As established earlier, project management literature is in the early stages of both quantitative and qualitative research and theory building. The review of marketing literature seems to be equally lacking in these critical areas. Bits and pieces of research, conceptual papers, and case reports, however, do not serve as a solid foundation on which to investigate the relationship of value to selling project management to senior executives. Fortunately, an extensive research report by the Economist Intelligence Unit (EIU) and IBM Global Services (EIU 1999, available at http://www.eiu.com in 2000) serves as a solid base on which to explore value alignment in selling services.

The EIU and IBM joined forces to develop a comprehensive framework to investigate the value of IT, with the intent of understanding how to sell IT products and services at the senior executive level. Essentially, this work aimed to help businesses differentiate between the different types and amounts of value that connect an organization's selling processes and activities with a buyer's value network (Delisle 2001). The resulting "value continuum" takes into consideration the perspective of buyers and sellers, and is adaptable for use in other industries to describe product/service promotion between firms.

The EIU and IBM sponsored research recognized the presence of four major areas of focus that they consider to exist along a continuum, where one side is not necessarily "better" than the other. Rather, the idea of the continuum is that the astute business is able to shift its value focus in anticipation, or at least in response, to market changes and/or economic crises, so that the types of projects it takes on make sound business sense. The major headings of the value continuum are broken into two areas, foundation and innovation values, under which two types of specific values are listed (EIU 1999):

Foundation Values

- *Efficiency*—Focus on core return on investment (ROI) and productivity goals, such as reducing costs, increasing quality, and cycle times.

- *Effectiveness*—Encompass customer service, collaboration, overall organizational effectiveness, knowledge sharing, and competency tracking.

Innovation Values

- *Market expansion*—Expand or create new markets, or develop a larger geographic or global presence.

- *Advantage creation*—Push the limits of organizational environments, changing industry, and market practices.

Tying the value continuum principles to the selling of project management helps one to understand the potential misalignment of buyer-seller goals, as well as the mismatched expectations about what the overall business strategy is trying to accomplish by using project management. The value continuum could assist sellers in identifying appropriate value propositions, and senior executives in making their assessments of the range of value and strategic advantage an organization has the potential of achieving by fully utilizing project management.

A modified version of the original framework served to focus our investigation into arguments and processes used in marketing and selling project management as a value-generating core competency, not an expensive overhead. Figure 2.1 presents a modified version of the original value continuum used in this study.

Buyer-seller business relationships, based on foundation values, involve tactical sales and purchases for quick-fix business solutions to generate profits and increase shareholder confidence. Focusing on this part of the continuum results in

Figure 2.1. Value Continuum (Adapted from EIU 1999)

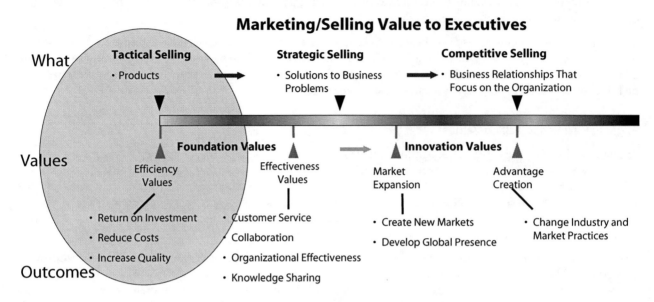

decisions made at the operational level of a firm, with minimal senior executive involvement. Decisions that only consider foundation-type values also do not critically examine the alignment between strategic directions and operational practices. As the relationship evolves, and the focus shifts towards effectiveness values, the emphasis may also shift to finding solutions to business problems—how does one make and keep the client or customer happy. Decisions rooted in effectiveness-based value generation essentially aim at improvements at the operational level of a firm, to help save the client time and money. Further to the right along the continuum into the innovation values, the emphasis definitely favors strategic business relationships that have the greatest potential to benefit both parties (buyers-sellers) over the long run. Decisions rooted in innovation values involve more senior executive involvement and, in most cases, a review of the alignment between strategic directions and operational practices.

As an organization shifts from left to right on the value continuum, they are essentially moving from more simple, straightforward relationships on the left side of the scale, which are grounded in economic and customer satisfaction selling arguments, to more complex relationships on the right side of the continuum, which involve more patience to develop, and perhaps a great deal more trust between seller and buyer to generate a type of synergistic partnership that diligent branding may enhance. The investment may be considered higher by senior executives the farther they shift to the right in the innovation value position, because the overall investment in more uncertain business initiatives may increase, as well as the anticipated payback. Similarly, sellers may dream of landing "the big one" that changes industry market practices. In reality, this effort may require ongoing persuasion to continually refresh the credibility and trust foundation of the buyer-seller relationship at the senior executive level. If branding has not been initiated, a long wait may ensue in capitalizing on the sale of project management. Research shows that firms that value and expect to achieve these kinds of results will be involved in relationships based on mutual trust and forbearance (Hartman 2000; Lesser 2000).

Marketing literature recognizes that buyers and sellers often have different value structures. The project management literature reviewed shows that valuing project management is an individual, and sometimes idiosyncratic, process. Being aware of differences may help sellers to understand the effort required to align buying and selling values, and that this alignment and its link to the management of expectations are likely two of the most critical aspects of successfully selling project management. With respect to values, senior executives are interested in how to measure and increase the return on their organization's investments. Traditionally, project management sales result from billing it as a method or technique to measure performance with the goal of increasing efficiency. Experience has shown that this tactical, operational focus produces mixed results in getting senior executive support for project management.

The review of the literature thus far has established that gaps in expectations and perceptions related to success, value, and project management help shape whether the buyer-seller relationship focuses on tactical or strategic outcomes. In short, senior executives focus on a more strategic or long-term view of value, but do not necessarily place equal importance on making investments in project management on the bases of softer, customer-related values or future benefits, as much as traditional financial arguments.

Organizational Theory Literature

Organizational theory covers a wide range of research and literature from leadership and organizational behavior to strategy and organizational structure. For this project, two relevant areas of organization theory research are strategic issues and sense making theory, both of which are introduced in this section.

Strategic Issues

Strategy researchers have explored how new strategic issues surface within individual organizations. Strategic issues are those that continuously appear on senior executives' radar screen as they develop corporate strategy and make management decisions (Dutton et al. 2000; Dutton and Ashford 1993; Dutton and Webster 1988; Dutton et al. 1997). As well, "issues are events, developments, or trends that have potential consequences for an organization" (Dutton and Webster 1988, 663). Issues have also been called wicked problems, as they are ill structured and less defined (Dutton and Ashford 1993). By studying managers' accounts of "issue selling" processes and their successful and unsuccessful efforts (called "issue selling" episodes), we can better understand the selling process (Dutton et al. 2000).

Senior executives often have little time to assess information and data that crosses their desks before they need to make decisions. Issues only become strategic if senior executives perceive them as being relevant to organizational performance (Dutton and Ashford 1993). This perception can engender buy-in from others within the organization, as there is a tendency to want to be part of a strategic issue that is positively received.

The theory on issue selling is limited, but it draws from social problem theory, impression management, and upward influence (Dutton and Ashford 1993). Top management tends to focus on issues that have been successfully legitimated as being important. In the case of project management, a key prevalent trend has been the high cost of project failures. Impression management views issue selling as a social process with tangible and intangible rewards for people. Relative to selling project management, sellers risk being associated with an issue perceived negatively, issues that fail or that stigmatize, thereby affecting their credibility (Dutton and Ashford 1993). Research in the area of upward influence looks at social persuasion and attitude changes from a social psychology perspective, as well as characteristics of the seller and buyer influencing the relative effectiveness of the attempts to influence (Dutton and Ashford 1993).

Issue sellers experience tensions that relate to doing whatever it takes to get an issue sold to curb behaviors, so that their credibility is not negatively impacted in the eyes of management. These tensions come up as they make choices on whether or not to initiate selling, how to package the issue, and what process to use to sell it (Dutton and Ashford 1993). In contrast, the marketing and selling literature uses elements of the Dutton categories in their prescribed strategies of selling to executives, but no article provides a comprehensive use of the type of framework put forth by Dutton (1993). The marketing literature also echoes many of Dutton's views, as he is one of the predominate sources of research in the area of seller credibility (Bistritz et al. 1999; Block 1991; 1992; Gardner and Bistritz 1998; Gardner, Bistritz, and Klompmaker 1996).

From the perspective of well-respected project management practitioners such as David Cleland, "Projects are the basic building blocks in the strategic management of products and services" (Cleland 1991, 19). Thus, senior executive attention to project management is related to who brings it to their attention, the credibility they have, and how it is presented (Dutton and Ashford 1993). Senior executives also pay attention to how strategic issues are framed (wording, emotional content). In addition, the selling process is a key factor. Thus, senior executive attention to project management, like other services, is also related to the selling process, e.g., who is involved, when, to what degree, and so on.

Dutton et al.'s (1997) work can also bring insight into selling project management by looking at several categories of issue selling practices. These include packaging, involvement, process, and contextual knowledge.

- *Packaging*—How is the issue presented, promoted, and bundled? Bundling means how the issue is tied to other issues or organizational goals. Was the service packaged well enough to communicate its value beyond the current project as a core competency to help the business meet strategic goals?

- *Involvement*—Who is involved in the selling process? Did the seller inform and keep senior executives updated about who is or could be involved as part of the sales team (seller credibility/trust issues)?

- *Process characteristics*—What was the formality of the process, how prepared was the seller, and what was the timing of the sell? Was the seller in tune with the comfort level of the senior executive who might be interested in investing in project management, was the sales person too assertive or not convincingly prepared, and was the argument timely in light of the business environment?

- *Contextual knowledge*—Did the seller know the people and how the organization works, as well as the company's plans and priorities (Dutton et al. 2000)? Has the seller made the commitment to build trust and credibility by getting to know the organization and its staff? Is the seller recognized in selling a trusted brand name?

Dutton et al.'s (2001) final contribution to this body of work explores the type of information in the sales context that is needed to devise appropriate sales arguments. They argue that sellers need three types of information. They need strategic information on the goals and objectives of the organization, coupled with normative information on "how things are done around here," and relational information about who plays important roles in decisions of these kinds and who needs to be involved. Most sellers do not gather all three of these types of information.

The key to selling project management in an organization is for sellers to understand how project management can become a strategic issue that gains senior executive attention in a positive way. The literature findings are particularly useful for the purpose of this study, because they help to elaborate the arguments and processes involved in selling project management to senior executives. Thus, this study uses the categories of processes, arguments, and context, as discussed, as a way to help shape the research direction.

Sense Making Approaches

The underlying roots of wicked problems, like mismatched expectations, are deftly explained by sense making theory (historical development documented in Weick 1996). The theory explores the processes that lay down the memories and experiences that individuals interpret and reinterpret. Sense making theory provides a way for project management, as a profession and an academic discipline, to look at processes of action and interaction that enable individuals to make sense of organizational activities. Thus, understanding processes and interactions from the perceptions of the seller and buyer may assist researchers in uncovering the underlying processes and practices that enable the sale of project management.

Research by Delisle (2001) and Thomas (2000) indicates that project management is not understood as a unitary and unambiguous concept in practice. This research sought support for the premise that difficulty in selling project management results in part from sellers trying to convey project management's business value using industrial-age tools and traditional financial metrics, including tactical selling approaches, whereas senior executives may be looking for very different value dimensions. For example, sellers and senior executives may understand the concept of project management and its value in very different ways, leading to gaps in sense making about project management as a whole. Those trying to market project management need to communicate values and benefits that are consistent with, and aligned to, the indicators senior managers use to evaluate such offering.

At a minimum, understanding selling and buying from the sense making point of view will help bridge gaps in conveying meaning about the value of project management at the senior executive level. Meaning, as understood in a social context, cannot be communicated, nor can the act of communication create meaning (Glanville 1997). Thus, no "correctness" ensues, "because individuals create their own meanings and only through agreements do parallel personal meanings develop" (Glanville 1997, 3). In short, sense making tells practitioners there is not likely a single best or correct way of selling to be identified. Rather, the creating of a shared meaning about the value of project management, and its capability to enable the successful delivery of projects, should be a key goal in establishing a useful buyer-seller relationship. This theoretical framework supports Dutton et al.'s contextualized descriptions of strategic issue selling, as discussed previously, and shapes the design of our research questions and data collection.

Translating Literature Review Findings into Action

This literature review drew our attention to key concepts that formed part of the theoretical foundation of what needed to be tested in this research study. How does one take these "fuzzy" concepts and decide what to examine, and prepare these concepts so that they can be operationally defined (made simple and succinct) and measured in empirical research?

The research team applied sense making processes to help complete this critically important set of tasks. To make a long story short, the key concepts coming from our analysis of the literature are revealed by the frequency of occurrence, outright emphasis by practitioners and researchers, and key findings from conceptual studies and empirical research. In research terms, these concepts form, and are represented as, "independent variables" to be measured in their research instruments. The following six independent variables (followed by a short explanation of what each one is getting at) form the core on which to build the data collection instruments for this study. The steps to measure them as part of the research process are presented in Chapter 3.

Study "Independent Variables"

- *Project management practices*—Assess processes, practices, and outcomes related to the effective use of the discipline.
- *Value of project management*—Compare foundation versus innovation values, tactical versus strategic, or operational versus strategic.
- *Seller credibility*—Assess self-judged and senior executive-judged credibility of the seller, seller demographics, and past project outcomes in the organization.
- *Initiation and packaging strategies*—Determine who brings project management to the attention of senior executives, what kind of credibility they have, timing, and how project management is presented.
- *Packaging processes*—Determine how selling arguments should be framed (wording and emotional content), what the value statements are, and how it could be bundled with other issues.
- *Selling processes*—Determine who is involved, what channels are used, and what the degree of formality is.

Particular attention will be paid to gaps in the understanding of the value and practice of project management among the three groups of interest—project personnel, consultants, and senior executives. These gaps are likely to highlight some of the barriers in selling project management to executives.

Summary

To summarize, this chapter presents the key findings from the literature review that we used to help establish a theoretical foundation for the research project. The literature review presents the higher level of knowledge about the three literature streams (project management, marketing/selling, and organization theory), and narrows the focus on points most relevant to the issue of selling project management. The chapter concludes with a brief overview of the process used to carry forth the knowledge extracted in the literature review to select and flesh out the key study concepts, which in research terms serve as the independent variables that are examined in this research.

The next chapter builds on this foundation by presenting the details of the research methodology. The project used a mixed-methodology approach, in that both qualitative and quantitative methods served to help makes sense of data collected for this research study.

CHAPTER 3

Study Methodology

This research project on selling project management to senior executives employed both qualitative and quantitative approaches. This chapter describes the overall research design and provides details on the methodologies used in each phase of the research.

Research Design Overview

The first phase involved a qualitative grounded theory approach to understanding the phenomenon of interest in this study. The second phase involved a large-scale survey and exploratory statistical analysis to generalize the findings to a large audience.

Phase I consisted of conducting a review of the marketing, project management, and organization theory literatures, developing interview protocols, conducting interviews, and analyzing the transcribed data. It was conducted from November of 1999 to September of 2000. The major research question in this phase was "Why is it difficult to sell project management to senior executives?" In preparing to answer this question, we studied concepts from the three bodies of literature, discussed in Chapter 2, and decided the best way to measure them. As presented in Chapter 2, these concepts essentially formed the "independent variables" that we tested in Phase II.

Phase II built on the findings of the first phase, as well as an additional literature review, to gather as much additional information about how senior executives view and value project management, as well as how practitioners and consultants sell it. The primary research question in this phase was "How do you successfully sell project management to senior executives?" The results of this phase allow for statistical generalizations. Phase II findings clearly validate the decision-making model involved in deciding to invest in project management derived from Phase I.

Full ethical review and approval of the intended conduct of the research investigation was obtained from the University of Calgary and Athabasca University. The informed consent process involved a letter to participants before they began the interview or survey. All respondents were given or able to print a copy of the letter for their records.

The next two sections provide more detail on the methodologies underlying each phase of the research to help readers understand the approaches used and the rigor with which the methods were applied. In both phases, the methodologies were chosen based on their ability to help answer the research questions.

Phase I Methodology

In Phase I, a grounded theory approach (Glaser and Strauss 1967; Strauss and Corbin 1990) suited the need to answer questions that were more exploratory in nature. Although the primary question revolved around finding out why it is difficult to sell project management to senior executives, as well as how is it successfully sold to senior executives, the underlying concepts needed to be revealed. By engaging in questioning from an inductive reasoning point of view (going from the specific instances to general conclusions), we could freely engage in the process of building theory. In contrast,

Table 3.1. Phase I Study Sample Frame

Sample Group	Brief Description
Senior executives (CEOs, CIOs, or vice presidents)	Individuals making decisions to purchase or not purchase project management (n = 10).
Project managers/practitioners (project management office managers, project managers, or directors of project management)	Those championing/selling project management largely in the context of their own organizations (n = 6).
External project management consultants/experts (smaller and larger independent sellers)	Experts whose experiences included both successful and unsuccessful attempts to sell project management to organizations (n = 9).

deductive reasoning starts with theory and uses hypotheses to test it. Through inductive reasoning "the researcher will develop theoretical propositions or explanations out of the data" (Mason 1998, 142).

To answer the open-ended research questions, we used mainly semi-structured interviewing techniques along with asking a few open-ended questions. Given the exploratory/qualitative nature of this phase of the study, no quantitative variables or dimensions were conventionally measured per se. We gathered information on key concepts suggested by the literature review that formed our initial theoretical foundation. In-depth exploration of these concepts generated a deeper understanding of selling project management, types of selling arguments presented, and types of processes pursued to sell or purchase project management. Fully expecting additional concepts to arise in the course of this process, we ensured careful examination of the quality of the data to keep track of emerging or repetitive themes and issues as the interviews progressed. The goal of this phase of the research was to develop a theoretically based understanding (embedded in real-life practice) of the arguments and processes involved in selling project management to senior executives.

Sampling Frame

A purposive "snowball" sampling technique was used to select participants based on their knowledge, skill, and expertise in project management. The initial participants were asked to provide contact information for two other senior executives whom they believed could contribute significantly to the study. These names were used to iteratively expand the sample size. Interviews were conducted with people representing organizations that had recently purchased project management services and those that had not, as well as those who had been successful, and those who had not, in selling these services to executives.

The research was conducted in Calgary, Alberta, a city that houses the second largest number of corporate head offices in Canada. The sampling technique initiated by contacting practitioners from the population of the Project Management Advisory Council (PMAC)—a group of project management experts whose membership represents committed companies that advise academics in the Project Management Specialization academic program at the University of Calgary. Council members are familiar with the program's research efforts at the University of Calgary, and they provide a wide perspective from different types of industries that employ project management. Phase I involved twenty-five participants that fit into one of three categories, as shown in Table 3.1.

Participants

Participants represented a diverse set of organizations producing various products and services, including oil and gas, healthcare, new product development, and information technology. In terms of age, 14 (61 percent) were between 36–46 years, and 9 (39 percent) were between 46–55 years. At the time of this research, two participants had their Project Management Professional (PMP®) certification and two were in the process of obtaining their certification. In general, the participants represented an experienced and educated group of senior executives, project personnel, and consultants.

Data Collection

The qualitative, semi-structured interviews required that participants answer between 30–35 semi-structured questions. Questions included ones like the following:

- What is project management?

- What is the value of project management to your organization?

- If you had to sell project management to your manager, colleague, or peer, how would you do it?

The complete interview protocol is in Appendix A. We pre-tested the questions with a panel of project management practitioners to ensure that each question was meaningful and capable of extracting the information needed to address the research questions. Two researchers were present for each interview in almost every case, to increase reliability and allow for validation of transcriptions. This duplication allowed the interviewers to review the interview findings and corroborate them with the interview experience. The interviewers taped each interview (with permission), and subsequent typed transcriptions of each interview (15–20 single spaced pages each) comprised the core data set to be analyzed in Phase I.

Data Analysis Strategy

The grounded theory approach also served as the primary way of making sense of the data collected from interviews in Phase I. In traditional grounded theory approaches (Glaser and Strauss 1967), researchers do not go into a study with preconceived notions and may only conduct a brief literature review. However, many authors utilize a modified grounded theory approach (see, for example, Thomas 2000), whereby a literature review of potentially related material serves as a foundation upon which to build. Considering the large gaps in the knowledge about selling project management and the scope of the work to be done, we chose this modified approach to develop the theoretical underpinnings of the challenges in selling project management to senior executives, and to understand the processes, contexts, and content before data collection.

Other than this difference, the data analysis proceeded according to recognized grounded theory approaches with "explanation and theory … fashioned directly from the emerging analysis of the data" (Mason 1998, 142). Our research followed protocol of grounded theory by paying attention to the emergence of themes as the interview progressed, and analyzing interview transcripts concurrently, so that patterns became clearer in an iterative manner as suggested by Strauss and Corbin (1990). The saturation point came by the fifteenth interview, when the interviewers began to see considerable consistency and redundancy in the themes, issues, and arguments emerging from the data. The subsequent analysis focused on identifying trends or themes related to successful implementation strategies.

Each interview was transcribed and then read carefully by all members of the research team. To help uncover and link themes and ideas, we used a computer assisted qualitative data analysis tool called ATLAS-ti version 4.2 (Scolari 1997) for the analysis. Atlas-ti software allowed the project team to code the data according to themes that emerged from the data. Coding was conducted on individual transcripts and also between transcripts when interlinkages were exposed. The transcripts still contain a vast array of information for further study on issues beyond the scope of this investigation.

In summary, data analysis consisted of five steps. First, all members of the researcher team read the transcripts and identified key themes and processes. Second, the researchers met as a group and came to consensus on the meaning and importance of the various themes identified. Third, these themes were summarized for each important question and for each participant in a Microsoft® Excel® spreadsheet that allowed us to compare themes across questions and participants. Fourth, the project team met again in person to "brainstorm" the linkages and challenges and discuss the relationships between the themes identified and the underlying selling processes. Finally, the research team drew linkages from discussions with relevant academic and practitioner resources to support and verify the validity of these preliminary findings.

Limitations

We drew a non-random sample from Calgary, Alberta. As well, the sample had predominantly more male participants than might be expected. Nonetheless, we achieved the qualitative research goal of developing a preliminary model on how project management is purchased in organizations, which served as a way to narrow the focus and construct a framework for Phase II. The results of Phase I lend themselves to analytic generalizations but not statistical ones, due to these limitations.

Phase II Methodology

The results from Phase I verified six key concepts related to selling project management, as presented in Chapter 2. These concepts serve as the independent variables that the Phase II study measured. To measure these variables, required the development of a questionnaire survey instrument. The foundation of these questions lay in conclusions coming from confirmation and challenges to the results initially examined, and interpretations of concepts generated from Phase I analysis, literature review findings, discussions with experts in the field, and examination of previous questionnaires on similar topics.

The survey targeted three specific areas of inquiry, including:

- Identifying and examining how project management is used in organizations at a strategic and operational level.

- Identifying the arguments and processes used to gain senior management attention for purchasing project management.

- Examining the demographic background of those involved, particularly with respect to their background preparation in project management.

The complete survey instrument is included in Appendix B. Appendix C contains summary results for each question.

Sampling Frame

The sampling frame for Phase II was a combination of convenience, purposeful, and random sampling from a number of key association sources. Administration of the survey online did not allow for strict random sampling, for example, posting requests for participation at key project management association sites solicited responses from the general project management population. The collection of demographic data served as a way to monitor the quality of data to prevent duplicate responses.

We worked with associations mostly representing project management personnel at the practitioner, consultant, and senior executive levels. The following associations allowed us either to post information about the study on their websites, have access to their emailing lists, or in some cases, issued the survey through their own administrative offices by email.

- Project Management Institute (PMI®)
- ESI-International
- Computers in Information Processing Society (CIPS)
- Professional Engineers of Ontario (PEO)
- CIO Canada Publications
- Athabasca University's Executive MBAs.

Specifically, CIPS provided a one-time only access to their entire emailing list and the rest of the organizations used random number generator techniques to provide us with a subset of randomly selected members; PEO only posted the survey on their website. CIPS, ESI-International, and PMI used a combination of survey email outs and website postings to promote the study and generate interest in participation. The range of organizations involved in our sampling frame allowed us to make generalizations mainly to North American project management practices and the information technology industry as a large subset.

Response Rates

Data collection via the online survey was conducted from 15 March 2001–16 April 2001. In total, 41,884 emails were issued to the study sample. Due to the changing nature of email addresses, the rejection rate (emails bouncing back unopened

Table 3.2. Response Rates by Organization

Organization	PMI®	ESI-Intl	CIO*	CIPS	PEO	AU	Total
Emails Sent	7,301	8,954	20,952	3,177	Website	1,500	41,884
Minus Bounce Backs**	6,206	7,610	17,808	2,700	NA	1,275	35,599
Responses	843	450	298	173	0	104	1,868
Response Rate	11.5%	5.0%	1.4%	5.4%	0%	6.9%	4.5%
Response Rate minus Bounce Back	13.6%	5.9%	1.7%	6.4%	0%	8.2%	5.3%

* Note that eliminating the very low response rate from the CIO mailout would substantially increase the response rate. However, CIO provided access to executive level input and so was included in the study.

** Using an estimate of 15 percent provided by one of the emailing lists, which is consistent with other similar studies.

and out of office replies) was approximately 15 percent. By continually tracking the number of emails that bounced during the data collection period, we were able to adjust the sampling frame. Thus, the delivered email invitations numbered approximately 35,600. Of these, 3,093 respondents accessed and completed the survey online, for a response rate of 8.7 percent. However, a fair number of these respondents eliminated themselves from further data collection by identifying their role in the company as non-project related. Thus, we collected 1,868 usable surveys, for a response rate of 5.3 percent overall. The survey has an accuracy rate of +/- 2.27 percent, 19 times out of 20.

Response rates by organization are depicted in Table 3.2.

This online survey enabled us to involve participants worldwide. However, we recognize that this approach eliminated those potential participants who do not have access to, or prefer not to, participate in electronically based surveys. The important trade-offs were the ease of administration, low cost, timeliness of data collection of an online survey, and convenience of completing the survey at the participant's convenience.

Electronic (email or online) surveys sometimes result in lower than anticipated response rates. However, current literature indicates that there is no consensus on what an acceptable response rate for Internet survey research designs is (Weible and Wallace 1998). Reports vary from 5–70 percent, with the lower number more common in attempts to generalize to wide population categories and the 70 percent more commonly reported for surveys within a company (Weible and Wallace 1998).

Calculation of response rates is not just a case of returned surveys versus no response. Most formulas do not take into account the complexities of research design, sampling process, and the practical difficulties of contacting and assessing potential survey participants (SISA 1999). This method could not be used in a website posting and email/Internet methodology, because the number of ineligible participants is not known at any given time. Furthermore, applying seven different formulas, recommended in various sources on statistics, to select an acceptable sample size (that will generate a reliable response rate) can still range from 35–400 respondents. The only consistency, with respect to calculation response rates in the literature, seems to be the variation (Hill 1998). This method appears simple; however, it does not take into account the complexities mentioned previously of research design, sampling process, and the practical difficulties of contacting and assessing potential survey participants (SISA 1998).

In conclusion, a response rate of 5 percent is low, but adequate to be able to make statistically valid generalizations about the study findings if the sample demographics seem to reflect the underlying demographics of the populations of interest. We confirmed that the sample was representative of the larger population by comparing demographics to find high face validity (match between research findings and what is going on in the real world). The demographics of our sample were examined with respect to personal and organizational demographics, and later compared to the demographics available from similar organizations and any other sources of representative demographics available. Thus, we are confident that the comparisons made truly show that the e-sample size is representative and the response rate allows for the generalization of findings to the broad project management community, including the types of organizations that provided the emailing lists used in the study.

Throughout the course of the study, in making decisions about methodology, including data collection and analysis, we applied the most stringent guidelines available. As well, the most conservative estimating techniques were also applied in the statistical analysis to increase the rigor. For example, the poorest response rates were from the PEO website and CIO mailing list. It could be argued that neither of these emailing lists attract the audience project management is particularly aligned with or that would help answer the research questions. Removal of all respondents from the overall response rate calculation dropped the response rate from almost 9 percent to 5 percent. However, since we had included these two sources in the actual distribution of email invitations to participate in the study, we did not delete them from the original sample size calculations.

Survey Logistics

A professional company was contracted to administer the survey online because they had proven experience with conducting international online surveys. SurveySite's™ (http://www.surveysite.com) role was to upload and post the survey and monitor response rates. This procedure enabled us to ensure participant confidentiality and ease of administration, since we did not have permission to send emails directly to participants in some cases. SurveySite™ also provided a preliminary descriptive report on the study findings, along with frequency results and the final data file of responses in the format of a Microsoft® Excel® spreadsheet. The data file was later converted to an SPSS® (version 10.0.7) data file. Information on SPSS® is available at http://www.spss.com/. SPSS® is a powerful academic and business statistical analysis software package. We used SPSS® for data screening, descriptive statistics, frequency calculations, and interpretive statistics such as correlations, exploratory factor analyses, and reliability testing.

Survey Structure

Over 100 questions formed the initial cut of the survey instrument. The research team independently reviewed the survey items and completed the survey, and modified the questions on multiple occasions. It was then pre-tested for validity and reliability using a panel of academic colleagues and project management practitioners. The sum of the pre-testing allowed for the reduction of questions to those most closely related to the research objectives and those that showed the highest reliability and validity. Criterion validity was addressed by using groups of questions (multi-measures) to reflect the key concepts (independent variables) instead of a single question (Cooper and Emory 1995). Content validity was addressed through the use of the literature review to identify the concepts, and through the use of a pilot test among academics to solicit their judgments.

The final instrument consisted of sixty-two questions, including seventeen questions on demographics and eleven open-ended questions. The survey used a behaviorally anchored, five-point Likert scale (with anchors, "strongly agree" and "strongly disagree"). The intermediate choices were "somewhat agree," "somewhat disagree," and "neither."

The survey questions reflected underlying concepts in three major areas of interest. The three areas of interest are shown in Figure 3.1.

The "Status of Project Management" questions explore the status of project management practice in organizations today. These questions examine project management practices in use, project outcomes, project manager preparation, and executive attention to project management.

The "Issues in Selling PM to Senior Executives" questions explicitly examine the issues in selling project management to senior executives, including the perceived value of project management, rates of success, successful arguments, and successful approaches.

The "Project Manager Preparation" questions explore project manager preparation in terms of demographics, levels of experience, levels of education, and demand for project management education.

Figure 3.1. Data Collection Areas

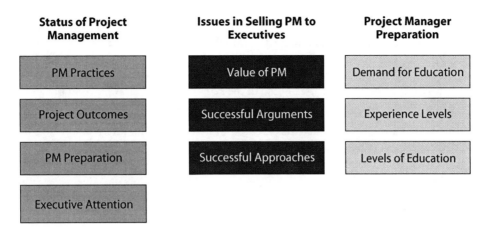

Status of Project Management	Issues in Selling PM to Executives	Project Manager Preparation
PM Practices	Value of PM	Demand for Education
Project Outcomes	Successful Arguments	Experience Levels
PM Preparation	Successful Approaches	Levels of Education
Executive Attention		

Phase II Statistical Analysis Strategy

Phase II data was subjected to a rigorous three-part process of statistical analysis. This section describes the steps involved in each part of the statistical analysis.

Part I—Data Screening and Instrument Reliability Testing

First, the data was screened and cleaned for any missing fields or misplaced coding using standard statistical tests. This cleaning was followed by descriptive analyses that confirmed that the data was within acceptable limits, i.e., the data was normally distributed and did not require transformations to prepare it for parametric analysis. In part, the normality of the sample was due to the robust sample size. The initial descriptive analysis also helped to identify trends in the data. Part one of the analysis involved demographic statistical analysis using Microsoft® Excel® and SSPS® statistical software package. Patterns from this analysis identified "hot spots" of key data to conduct further analysis.

Next, we addressed instrument reliability by testing the internal consistency, or the degree to which the survey instrument reflects the underlying concepts important to this research. The study applied a Chronbach Alpha (α) of 0.60 accuracy, as suggested in Cooper and Emory (1995) as the lower level of acceptability. Note that often social science research of an exploratory nature aims for 0.40, which is considered as an acceptable cut off. Chronbach's Alpha is a measure of the internal consistency of questions, based on average inter-item (question) correlations. A high alpha value means that other researchers can have confidence that they will obtain similar results. Questions that did not meet the stated alpha coefficient were eliminated from subsequent analysis in part two of the data analysis before the Exploratory Factor Analysis (EFA). Eliminating questions with "low alphas" also helped avoid "cross-loading problems" in the EFA, where all factors seem to be important in selling project management.

Part II—Correlational Analysis

Next, the data underwent correlational analysis to further identify relationships, trends, and associations between study variables. Reliability issues were addressed, as discussed further into the next section. This part also included scrutinizing the data on participant demographics (position, industry, and country) conducting both descriptive and inferential statistical analysis (comparisons between demographics and the three types of data collected) to gain insight into the actions involved in making selling project management to senior executives an easy or tough sell.

Part III—Exploratory Factor Anlaysis

Part three of the analysis involved EFA to reduce and summarize the data, to first identify the top factors explaining how project personnel and consultants sell the discipline to senior executives. The EFA also allowed us to generate different theoretical models and see how the data best fit with the objectives of the study.

The EFA analysis was conducted on a split-half sample. Although the entire data set was used for the initial descriptive statistical analysis, we used the split-half method to prepare the data for the EFA. The sample size and response rate were large enough to split the usable data set into two halves, as recommended in the split-half technique by Hill (1998) and Cooper and Emory (1995). The data set was randomly divided into two halves, with one-half serving as the basis for the statistical analysis in Phase II, and the other half being reserved for validation/corroboration of findings and interpretations at a later date. As well, the split halves were useful in comparing factor matrices and assessing the robustness of the solution across the sample (Hill 1998). The split half used in the actual data analysis resulted in the following numbers of participants for each of the three study groups: 499 project personnel, 244 consultants, and 190 senior executives.

Exploratory factor analysis is a multivariate statistics method to determine data interrelationships between the study concepts (independent variables) (Cooper and Emory 1995). An EFA is an interdependence technique to reduce and summarize large volumes of data, meaning it allows researchers to derive the smallest number of explanatory concepts that are the most powerful in explaining how to sell project management. In research terms, these concepts refer to the "maximum amount of common variance." The result is a set of "factors" that is most useful in helping to explain the issues surrounding selling project management.

From this point, the goal is to reveal underlying combinations or patterns of the concepts (independent variables) that have the greatest explanatory power. In research terms, this goal refers to the concepts that explain the highest percentage of the overall variance. To accomplish this task, we applied Principal Component Analysis (PCA) to the factor analysis outputs to transform these set of factors into "composites" or "models" (Cooper and Emory 1995). The models show the key patterns in the relationship among concepts, although the models cannot show that one concept causes the other to increase or decrease. Thus, the interpretations of the data tell the seller that they need "more" or "less" of each type of argument or process in selling. To summarize, PCA is a data reduction technique that identifies the key independent variables from a larger set of variables, as well as creating "new" combinations of concepts to form independent variables, while still retaining the nature and characteristics of the original variables. All this effort is necessary to be able to come up with a set of key concepts that are grouped together in ways that reveal the process of selling project management.

By applying PCA, the data is transformed into a parsimonious set of models that help make sense of the relationships in the data collected in survey questions 2–12. In short, the EFA, as a whole, allows us to identify the key factors—those with the greatest ability to explain the variance—and the patterns in how project personnel and consultants sell the discipline to executives.

Detailed Description of Data Screening and EFA Analysis[1]

Multiple EFAs on different subsets of data always begin with running descriptive statistics to "screen" the data set. This action involves looking for any nonparametric correlations and checking reliability values. As well, a number of tests help prepare the most rigorous data set. Each is introduced and then described in this section. The tests included a sphericity test, the Kaiser-Meyer-Olkin (KMO) test (refers to a measure of sampling adequacy), and anti-image test (for Measures of Sampling Adequacy [MSA]). This latter test was done as a confirmation to eliminate survey questions that had low Chronbach Alphas.

Bartlett's sphericity assessment tests for the presence of correlations among the study concepts. Values increase with sample size, and become significant if the output reads 0.000. Very small values (less than 0.05) indicate that there are probably significant relationships among the variables. A test value higher than 10 indicates that the data is not suitable for factor analysis. All our results from the Bartlett's test were significant, thus the next step was to run the KMO test.

The KMO statistic indicates which concepts (independent variables) represent the "common variance," i.e., which might be best in helping to explain the underlying issues examined in the research questions. High values (close to 1.0) generally indicate that this data may be confidently useful in conducting a factor analysis. If the value is less than 0.50, the results of the factor analysis probably will not be very useful. Thus, scores greater than 0.50 are considered adequate and 0.60 or higher, even better (Garson 2002).

All results for the eight groups that were analyzed show KMO values of greater than 0.70, except for the two groups having fewer respondents (Very Successful Consultants, n = 38; Very Unsuccessful Project Managers and Consultants, n = 19).

MSAs are then determined by the KMO test values, showing a range of 0.80 for each of the three groups, as recommended by Hair et al. (1998). Question items with MSAs lower than 0.5 were not included in the factor analysis. This test was repeated several times using rotated component matrices to avoid multicollinearity, and the results were scrutinized to help us determine if we needed to delete additional items from the next iteration of the EFA. Only the resulting data reflecting high MSAs were used to run the final reported iteration of the EFAs.

With respect to multicollinearity (confounding of concepts making it difficult to know which factors are truly important in selling), a certain level is necessary and acceptable because the objective is to identify interrelated variables. However, too much is not necessary or acceptable, because it indicates the factors are not orthogonal (truly independent of each other). Factors with multicollinearity, also known as "cross loading" in research terms, of 0.40 or higher were deleted from subsequent iterations in the EFA process.

The square of the factor loadings (results of an iteration) represents the amount of total variance explained, or ability of each factor to explain the issues in the research questions. For example, a value of 0.50 squared means that 25 percent of the variance is explained by that particular factor that represents the concept being measured. Factor analysis involves an element of judgment. Initial iterations with less stringent cut-off values produced factors with components with three or fewer items. However, this type of exploratory, iterative analysis helps the research team build a more thorough understanding of the data, even if these earlier efforts are not included in the final report. The last two iterations of the EFA used factor loadings of 0.80 and 0.70, where a cut off of 0.70 would account for 50 percent of the variance (when squared). The last iteration used a 0.60 cut off to capitalize on the use of EFA to build theory. Thus, too stringent of a cut-off point would eliminate some factors that were intriguing and of interest, but did not meet the most rigorous cut off of 0.70.

The tables in Chapter 6 present the final results of the factor analysis. These values meet the 0.70 cut off in most instances, with those scores meeting the 0.60 cut off highlighted in light gray. Factors having the highest scores are shown in dark gray. Factor loadings of 0.80 or higher are extremely difficult to obtain, however, we do show some values in this range in the tables.

The reason for the elaborate process described in this section is based on the need to achieve clean separations between factors. The next task was to determine the number of factors to extract to account for as much of the variance as possible, meeting the established rigor. In short, what factors can help us answer our research questions most effectively. In social sciences, the common practice is to either use a "rule of thumb," where solutions that extract 60 percent of the total variance are reported, or use Eigenvalues and Scree tests. We used all three approaches.

Eigenvalues are the column sum of squared loadings for a factor. They report the latent roots (or factors not directly measured in the study) and the variance accounted for by each. In other words, how much of the explanation about selling project management lay in concepts that came out of the data, but were not necessarily measured directly as a key concept? Only latent values greater than one were considered acceptable.

Scree tests then plot the latent roots against the key concept measured (which are represented by factors meeting the cut offs described in the previous paragraphs) to provide an even more stringent way of discriminating which latent factors met the cut-off value of one. We decided to use the latent variables from the Scree tests.

Resulting EFA Models

The final EFA results represent a set of findings that meet strict cut-off criteria for rigor. In presenting the results in Chapter 6, the first factor portrays the strongest correlation. Namely, it is the most powerful in explaining the particular concept examined. Subsequent factors follow in the order of their explanatory ability. The term "factor" refers to the sets of items (or questions on the survey), in order of priority, that produced the strongest results. The EFA produces factors, but does not name them. Thus, each factor was given a brief descriptive name that related to its content.

Since the analysis included the breakdown of the factor models by the three groups of interest, we were able to identify common core successful selling practices, and common core very successful selling practices. Further subdivision ensued as the analysis progressed to identify the level of success by group. The resulting eight models are identified in this chapter (Table 3.3), and

Table 3.3. Model Names and Relationship to Groups

Model #	Model Name	Sample Size	Included Group(s)
1	GENERAL SELLING BASE MODEL	n = 743*	All project personnel and consultants
2	PROJECT PERSONNEL SELLING MODEL	n = 499	Project personnel only
3	CONSULTANT SELLING MODEL	n = 244	Consultants only
4	VERY SUCCESSFUL SELLING BASE MODEL	n = 99	Project personnel and consultants
5	VERY SUCCESSFUL PROJECT PERSONNEL MODEL	n = 61	Project personnel who reported being very successful in selling only
6	VERY SUCCESSFUL CONSULTANT MODEL	n = 38	Consultants who reported being very successful in selling only
7	VERY UNSUCCESSFUL SELLING MODEL	n = 19	Project personnel and consultants who reported being very unsuccessful in selling project management
8	SENIOR EXECUTIVE MODEL	n = 190	Senior executives only

* Note all of the exploratory factor analysis was conducted on one-half of the data to allow for future testing of the models derived on the remaining data.

fully explained in Chapter 6 in the order in which they were developed, to help the reader follow the description of the process of model building. The model "labels" are shown in capital letters to help the reader easily find them in the text.

The project personnel group plus the consultants group forms the GENERAL SELLING BASE MODEL (n = 743, based on 249 + 244). This base model is used in drawing out common core selling practices and making initial comparisons between the very successful project personnel and the consultants, as well as comparing the very successful data files to the very unsuccessful data files. Finally, we compared all the results to what the senior executives explained they were looking for when they decided to invest or purchase project management services. The comparisons and contrasts between the different data models are reported in Chapter 6.

Generalizability of Results

How do researchers test the sample for normality to ensure it represents the larger population? The Kolmogorov-Smirnov test measures the sample normality, to confirm that the sample comes from a normal distribution, allowing for confidence in traditional statistical analysis (Cooper and Emory 1995). As well, sample size must be considered in determining how confident the larger population can be in accepting these results. As established in this report, the research is based on an adequate sample size. Advanced statistical testing of between 50–100 observations, as in this research, follows a research "rule of thumb"—having a minimum of 5 times the number or observations as there are concepts (or testable independent variables). This study had 1,868 participants, which resulted in testing 60 independent variables for a case-to-variable ratio of 31. Thus, the general case model did not suffer from "over-fitting"—pushing the explanatory power of the data beyond the capability of the sample size, which is a common problem. As well, the split half used for the EFA still met the constraints of the rule of thumb to allow for generalizability. However, as each subsequent model had less cases associated with it, the generalizability of the results becomes less clear. For the models with particularly low representation (the VERY UNSUCCESSFUL SELLING MODEL, for instance) in our sample, the results are not generalizable and are presented here for interest and to generate future research areas.

Summary

To summarize, this chapter presents an overview of the study methodology including a description of the steps in Phase I and Phase II of the study. This overview included presentation of information about the population of interest, the study samples, sampling techniques, limitations, data collection instruments, response rates, analysis strategies, reliability, and generalizability. The next three chapters address the findings from Phase I and Phase II, beginning with Phase I.

Notes

1. This material is included for researchers and others interested in the mechanics of the statistical analysis. For most readers, this level of understanding of the statistical methods is not necessary.

CHAPTER 4

Phase I Findings: Why Is It Difficult to Sell Project Management to Senior Executives?[1]

This chapter presents key interpretive findings from the first phase of the research project. As established in previous chapters, the primary research question for this phase of the study was "Why is it difficult to sell project management to senior executives?" First, we explored the participants' understanding of project management and identified any gaps that may exist in understanding value and selling/buying project management. This initial step allowed us to identify and examine the process of selling project management and the interaction patterns between the buyer and seller.

Understandings of Project Management and Its Value

A Guide to the Project Management Body of Knowledge (PMBOK® Guide) – 2000 Edition calls a project "a temporary endeavor undertaken to create a unique product, service, or result" and defines project management as "the application of knowledge, skills, tools, and techniques to project activities to meet project requirements" (PMI 2000, 204–205). Participants' definitions of projects and project management closely coincided with these terms, in that interviewees used words that were similar. This finding is particularly interesting given that only four of the twenty-five individuals interviewed had any formal relations with the Project Management Institute (PMI®), and yet the definitions were quite widely held. These definitions are tactical in that they relate to tools, techniques, and skills. They also referred to simple value statements of either meeting or exceeding expectations. Consistent with these definitions, the approach to selling project management was also tactical. None of the participants initially described project management as a philosophy and no one referred to specific project management methodologies. In general, participants had a fairly consistent, "shared," albeit basic, understanding of project management.

Further questioning revealed a more diverse understanding of particular aspects of project management. Though some participants viewed it as a tool or technique, others viewed it as a lifestyle, a part of their belief system. It was also described in religious terms on more than a few occasions, with practitioners stating that they had "found the religion of project management," and describing themselves as "converts." The majority of senior executives provided less passionate or detailed responses. They described project management as conceptual, or as a tactical toolbox for getting things done. The consultants were the only group that described project management in strategic terms such as "a core understanding or belief," and as "scalable, flexible, and related to shareholder value."

The value of project management varied widely across our three groups. To project managers, its value related to its efficiency and effectiveness in helping them with their track records and career paths. As such, they focused on tactical strategies in selling project management (features and attributes), because these were the values of importance to them. One described it as an "insurance policy." Another described it as having the right people do the right thing at the right time. Many related its value to the iron triangle of "time, cost, and scope." To many in this category, the value of project management was so obvious it almost did not bear explaining.

Figure 4.1. Project Management Understanding and Value Matrix

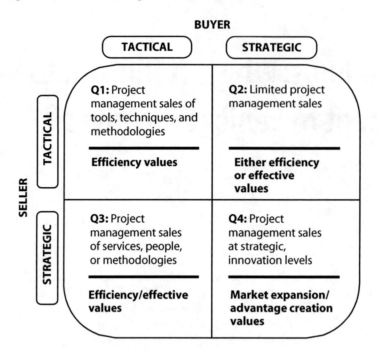

Large-scale consultants valued project management for its contribution in increasing revenue through sales and establishing their presence on accounts. They preferred to focus on strategic level outcomes to sell project management; however, they were willing to focus on whatever benefits the client wanted to buy. Small-scale consultants were also interested in revenue and tended to sell project management benefits tactically, relative to their individual skills and expertise, and the perceived needs of senior executives.

The value of project management to senior executives related to their company becoming more efficient and effective in its business capacities and, ultimately, a personal benefit of advancing their careers. They wanted to buy services that were aligned to their strategic business and professional goals. In most contexts, they were more interested in buying tools or techniques that impacted strategic outcomes than tactical project management solutions aimed at improving or sustaining innovative business operations. However, in crisis situations, project management problems are often elevated to the strategic level (when they really do not belong at that level) and senior executives become more willing to listen to sellers, even to those still selling tactically.

In all the interviews conducted, only those interviewed from one projectized firm consistently described project management as providing strategic benefits. All others interviewed described it as a corporate tactic. The rationale given was that business priorities lay elsewhere. As such, project management was viewed as a competence for most of those interviewed, while it was viewed more strategically at the one projectized firm.

Summarizing these findings on the meaning and value of project management and in the context of the value continuum described in Chapter 2, we note that the participants report using efficiency and effectiveness values in different combinations. They believed that these combinations helped them to relate to their overall strategic or tactical understanding of project management (EIU 1999). These relationships are depicted in Figure 4.1. Note that the ideas in this figure are shown in a similar figure in previous publications.

Figure 4.1 depicts the relationship between respondent's perceptions—how they perceive the meaning and value of project management in relation to buyers and sellers. In Quadrant 1 (Q1), project management is understood in tactical terms by both buyers and sellers, and purchased for efficiency values, such as return on investment, reduced costs, and increased quality. Although the emphasis is on tools and techniques, the relationship is still aligned between the buyer and seller. Most project management sales relationships identified in the study belong to this quadrant.

In Quadrant 2 (Q2), buyers act strategically and most sellers, if not all, act tactically. In this case, buyers will seek out sellers that are aligned to their values. The issue of trust and credibility of the seller plays an important role in gaining entry for the sale, and also generating the potential for repeat sales.

In Quadrant 3 (Q3) where buyers are tactical and sellers are strategic, senior executives that purchase project management services may come to realize the added value of doing so, but possibly at the risk of resistance to change within lower levels of the organization, as project management is introduced at a more advanced level. Those selling strategically to tactical buyers and those selling tactically to strategic buyers (Q2, Q3) might find that they are not aligned and either they adapt their sales strategies accordingly or are given even less access to senior management.

Those selling strategic solutions will be aligned with buyers seeking effectiveness values (customer satisfaction, collaboration, organizational effectiveness, and knowledge sharing). Quadrant 4 (Q4) is similar to Q1 in that there is alignment. The seller and buyer (Q4) understand the need to use project management for long-term success from an organizational and business standpoint. Buyers seek innovation values like market expansion (creating new markets or developing a global presence) and advantage creation (changing industry and market practices) (EIU 1999). Sellers in this quadrant focus on relationships at the business-to-business level. We found only one such case at a firm where we interviewed projectized staff.

Barriers to Selling Project Management

The feedback on barriers to successful project management experiences indicated that project managers and senior executives do not realize the strategic value of project management beyond its role as a control mechanism. This limited view leads to the dismissal of project management as expensive overhead that has a negative impact on business value creation.

Out of the senior executives interviewed, several stated that project management was "easy and something anyone can do." Of the six practitioners, several cited resistance to purchasing project management as a lack of alignment between stakeholders' perceptions, as well as a lack of willingness to "put some skin on the table" and share in the project risk. The "skin" in question is the senior executive's unwillingness to make a real tangible commitment. Still others indicated that some senior executives lacked a clear understanding of project management, and that they viewed it as expensive overkill. One practitioner stated, "These people don't know project management, they don't trust it, and they think it is 'make work.'" The results showed that within the buyers' domain, there is a wide range of opinions and attitudes toward project management.

Similarly, a number of the consultants believed that senior management did not understand project management or its true potential. Some indicated that senior executives did not understand what it takes to do projects well, nor did they appreciate the detail involved in project management. They believed that this hurdle could only be overcome by a change in the mindset of senior management, with an accompanying change in organizational culture.

One key issue appears to be a mismatch or disconnect between needs and expectations. That is, project managers do not always use the right arguments to convince senior management. Thus, disconnects occur between the project managers and the senior executives, because the project managers tactically sell the features and attributes (merits) of specific tools and techniques for the success of the project to senior executives, and senior executives want results and benefits at the business or corporate level (e.g., increase in shareholder value). Therefore, project managers need to convince senior executives of the value of project management by going well beyond the traditional metrics of delivering on time, on budget, and within scope, to selling its merits on a much wider scale. This change will require project managers to first get a good grasp on what they do, in order to make the right connection between project management and business objectives, before expecting senior executives to change the way they view and support project management.

How Is Project Management Successfully Sold?

To answer this question, we asked participants to tell us the story of a time when they were involved in the "purchase" or "sale" of project management within an organization. A synthesis of the stories resulted in the common decision points

Figure 4.2. Context—Common Types of External Triggers

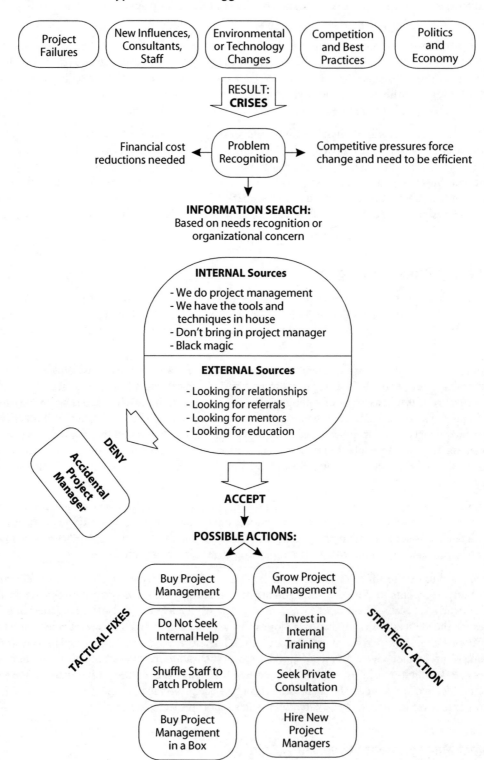

for Figure 4.2 and the discussion following. Figure 4.2 presents a flow chart of issues that the results suggest are present in senior executives common need-based, decision-making processes for buying project management.

As shown in Figure 4.2, the decision-making process may be driven by underlying triggers that are lying dormant until the timing is right to ignite a crisis within a particular organization. Once in crisis mode, the organization seeks out reasons for, and tries to make sense of, the problem. This problem recognition is driven internally by needing to streamline costs, or externally, by recognizing the need to keep in front of the competition.

The problem recognition then leads to an information search activity. This search marks a key place for seller involvement, because the senior executive may seek information inside the organization or turn to external consultants. Internally, at this stage, senior executives may run into the types of arguments presented in Figure 4.2. Alternately, or in response to this information, the senior executive may seek to build relationships, look for referrals for specialists, seek advice from mentors, or look for high impact courses/seminars to quickly get up to speed.

Another key place in the process lies in the decision of the senior executive to deny or accept that serious crises and underlying issues exist. In a denial situation, the decision is made to maintain the status quo and "weather the storm." Staff may be shuffled to the project manager positions, although they are not given any training, support, or pay increases. Hence, the appearance of the "accidental project manager."

If the decision is to accept that improved project management is the solution to the problem situation, the senior executive has made a first step to bridge the knowing-doing gap. Hence, the senior executive must commit to doing something, as well as taking action to mitigate the problem. Actions may include growing project management in house by investing in training and education of project management staff, hiring new fully prepared project managers, or seeking consultation to further deploy resources, which are all strategic in nature because their benefits go beyond the crises. Conversely, the senior executives may initiate actions of a more tactical nature, including buying project management software or consultant methodology templates, acting like they are seeking help, but actually doing nothing to fix the problem in reality, or shuffling staff to make the problem "go away."

Interestingly, not one interviewee mentioned that project management was successfully sold proactively, as a strategic investment, as supported by Block (1991; 1992). In organizations not rife with crises, senior executives seem less inclined to spend money on project management, due to the perception that it is expensive overhead (Ibbs and Kwak 2000). This reality explains some of the frustrations and challenges internal project managers faced in their efforts to sell project management proactively.

The interviewees indicated that the triggers to buy project management were related to a combination of external and internal factors as reactions to specific needs, e.g., competition for market share, environmental changes, and internal crises (Sawy et al. 1999). Internally (personally and organizationally), the decision to buy project management primarily related to the rescue of an extremely troubled, failing/failed project, or the advent of mega/complex projects. These forces appear to influence the value creation process and in turn, the very core of how a business functions. The impact of these contexts left the companies feeling that they were in "organizational crisis" situations.

Specifically, crises forced senior executives to consider the merits of project management in terms of the business problem. Recognition that the firm needed to improve the project management processes was usually based on the "insurance policy" value of project management in reducing risk and buying them certainty, or its contribution to their personal success. Senior management's "willingness to pay" for project management was associated with their perception of the pay off—total revenue must exceed total cost. They tend to avoid buying project management because the tangible benefits are not immediately evident, especially on larger projects that take a longer amount of time.

Conversely, "willingness to accept" the loss of project management as an option/strategy in the future became much more of a compensation issue that places the loss on a grander economic scale.[2] For example, senior executives may be willing to pay modest sums for project management as an initial capital investment. However, the numbers may skyrocket when asked what they are willing to accept, in terms of economic compensation, for the loss of the opportunity to purchase project management in the future (especially in a crisis situation). In practice, if a project manager pulls a high-profile project out of the fire and/or makes the company a significant capital gain, then based on this experience, a senior executive would highly value the opportunity to use project management again. In this case, the senior executive would be willing to pay a relatively higher price to ensure that adequate project management exists on the next project. Once the senior executive recognizes the value of project management, the threshold of valuation increases. In either case, the decision may hinge on only one variable (typically cost), without reference to future opportunities over time, which acts to underestimate, or sometimes overestimate, the definition of the value of project management.

Following the information search process, firms may take action to either buy project management services or develop it internally. Decisions at this stage to buy project management services are often triggered by crises. Senior executives tend to reach out to specific project management consultants based on prior relationships or referrals, e.g., those that were "top of mind" for specific services or skills. Rarely did the senior executives report seeking out new relationships with consultants or establishing stronger ties with internal advocates of project management.

The results suggest three reasons internal sources of information are not cultivated. First, senior executives tended to view consultants with a different degree of credibility (often a higher level) than their own project managers. In many cases, the organizational crisis was in response to internal poor performance on projects. Project managers were usually held accountable when projects were in trouble, and senior managers failed to appreciate the element of shared responsibility (Jugdev and Hartman 1998). This situation tended to reduce the credibility of project management proponents within the organization at the very time when senior executives might be ready to invest in it.

Second, another challenge that internal project proponents faced in selling to their senior executives related to power and language. Typically, project management proponents were not on a similar level in the hierarchy and so did not have access to resources, influence, and coalitions, and did not share a common business strategy language with the senior executives. When project managers focused on project minutiae, senior executives stopped listening.

Third, senior executives often got mixed messages from their internal resources, as these messages were at times in conflict with those offered by the consultants. Generally, internal project managers reply to senior executive queries about the state of project management in the organization in one of the following ways:

- "We do project management and we do it well, so we don't need help." This reaction reflects a resistance to change and exemplifies denial in terms of project management problems and potential improvements.

- "We don't need project management. We have managed to do projects 'the old way' for years and do not need to change our practices or learn new ways." This reaction reflects a resistance to change, as well as a lack of awareness of the value of the project management discipline.

- "We need help with project management. Thank goodness we are receiving help and our concerns are finally being heard." This level indicates a heightened level of awareness that improvements are possible.

Senior executives receiving the first two types of responses are likely to be either confused or angry since they recognized the problems related to suboptimal project management practices. Senior executives receiving the third type of response are not likely to turn to this group for advice, as they are perceived to have been the root causes of problems to begin with, and not a source of expertise to draw on.

In this situation, those seeking to promote project management are severely handicapped by the tendency of senior executives to explore an investment in project management only in crises. Clearly, this group needs to develop better ways of gaining access and promoting interest in project management as a support to business objectives.

Buying-Selling Process

Once the need was recognized and heightened awareness of project management achieved, it usually led to the acceptance of project management as a potential solution. Then, senior executives took action by either buying project management externally from consultants or growing it internally by training their staff, hiring project managers, and augmenting this strategy with some consulting services. These two choices differ in that buying project management services reflects an organizational culture that views it as a commodity. On the other hand, those companies that grow it internally are more likely to support it as a core competency. These companies indicated that it took years to grow project management internally and that the progress was incremental.

Figure 4.3. Buyer-Seller Relationships in Organizations

	BUYER	
	TACTICAL	**STRATEGIC**
SELLER — TACTICAL	**Q1:** Unstable relationships forming to solve crises	**Q2:** No relationship
SELLER — STRATEGIC	**Q3:** Unstable relationship—allows for dramatic change event to shift value beliefs	**Q4:** Project management sales of services, people, or methodologies

In cases where the need for project management continued to be denied at this stage, the practitioners believed that there would be no change. In these organizations, project management was viewed as simply something anyone could do when the need arose. In such companies, project managers were often promoted up the technical ranks and awarded the title "project manager," although they did not necessarily have the actual experience or formal training to fill the role effectively. One interviewee used the term "accidental project manager" to describe these individuals.

Based on participant information and literature, we developed the following model that delineates the way project management is sold/bought in organizations. Figure 4.3 depicts the buyer-seller relationship in organizations. The concepts for this figure are taken from previous publications, but are presented differently to facilitate the discussion here.

Traditionally, project management sales relationships follow the trend shown in Quadrant 1, where tactical relationships focused on selling features of a business solution. Buying occurred at a reflexive or involuntarily level, such that no real learning took place. If the seller does not "elicit" the desired response, then no relationship could be established (Quadrant 2). If the seller elicited the desired response, a dysfunctional relationship might be established, such that no new behaviors are learned; instead, associations are developed through pairing previous experiences with associations made in response to the belief that one has control over the external trigger events.

Currently, practitioners are selling tactically, yet expecting strategic respect. This approach creates a situation whereby actions and behaviors contradict each other and change feels chaotic, like the whirl of a tornado, as shown in Quadrant 3. In order to affect change that resonates on a personal and organizational level, strategic selling, as well as buying, must occur, as shown in Quadrant 4. Only at this level will sustainable and true learning take place.

As an intermediary step, sellers may initially reach buyers on a tactical level, as shown in Quadrant 3. The responsibility for where the relationship goes from there rests with the seller and buyer being honest about the benefits of the relationship, rather than pushing the features of the project management solution. Features refer to the quick-fix attributes of a tool or technique, whereas benefits refer to the business outcomes at a strategic level. As a strategist, the seller moves the buyer into an area of trust that is conducive to making personal and organizational changes. The seller can begin to identify how the business solution relates to internal issues (things that keep the executive up at night) as "controllable" trigger events. Buyers can begin to see the futility of reacting reflexively or trying to control external trigger events, such as market volatility and politics, and focus instead on more positive initiatives to promote project management.

Quadrant 4 shows a healthy, sustainable relationship whereby new behaviors are learned. Sellers and buyers do not act based on past associations from failed or successful experience. Rather they jointly tell a story that makes sense, because it reflects the joint values of each party. Both parties learn the desired behaviors instead of reflecting on what they perceive each other to want. The benefits of a mutually responsive relationship become evident, helping both parties realize their respective goals.

Our findings suggest that disconnects exist between what sellers promote and what buyers want to hear regarding project management. A naiveté appears around the belief that project management should be valued for its own sake. Thus, senior executives fail to see project management's value connection with the goals of the organization. In addition, the "sale" of project management, at present, appears to be a response to internal crises or changes in the environment instead of a proactive business decision. Those interested in being more effective at selling project management will benefit from learning and applying the basics of marketing strategies, listening to their target audience, and ensuring that they align the sale of project management to match the executive's degree of receptiveness on the value continuum.

Selling project management to senior executives requires project managers to learn different skills and overcome the discomfort of acting in a "sales" capacity. Project managers' experience with project management means that they best understand its value and benefits within their company. They appreciate its value and benefits when it is used effectively on projects and they appreciate its need when projects do not go well. Project managers are excellent ambassadors to promote project management in business terms to senior executives. They can develop skills in putting forth arguments about how project management benefits organizations. They can do this by applying best practices and heightening senior management awareness of the value and benefits project management can add to realizing their business imperatives.

As with any project, the attempt to sell project management at the executive level benefits from careful planning and preparation. The results of Phase I provide some insights into the process necessary to sell project management and some of the arguments that others have found to be successful.

Phase I Insights

Phase I findings suggest that the difficulty in selling project management at the executive level often results from cognitive gaps in the marketing relationships. For example, project managers sell features and attributes when senior executives want to hear about results and benefits. At times, project managers and consultants are guilty of selling before the need has been identified, let al.one agreed upon, by senior executives. These disconnects could be viewed as misalignments between values and expectations. Those involved in selling project management to senior executives can benefit from understanding and applying some basics tenets from marketing and communication (e.g., improving their listening skills in terms of learning how to frame the problem senior executives want answered). This approach will enable them to make the right connections about what senior executives are receptive to hearing in business terms. We suggest using a three-point approach of triggers, responses, and proof to explain project management benefits.

Trigger

Understand what the triggers to buy are for senior executives. Currently, the strongest triggers for the need to buy project management at the executive level appear to be related to issues that result in an external crisis or negative project activity. A trigger may be an event or situation that puts pressure on a place, event, or person within the organization, or the environment may become unstable (i.e., market crash). This trigger ignites and creates "crisis mode" in the organization. Buying occurs at a reflexive or involuntary level associated with current problems and no real learning takes place. This behavior relegates project management to a reactive fast fix. This cycle perpetuates itself on the underlying belief that project management will help control and diffuse external trigger events. From a sales perspective, this behavior means that sales will always be reactive. However, until we determine how best to sell project management at the strategic level, project management proponents need to be ready to respond to external triggers.

To increase the potential for proactive sales, project managers can initiate the trigger by focusing on questions like: "What are the top five things the executive is trying to do for the company?" "What are their priorities?" and "What keeps them up at night?" Listen for clues and insights into these areas. Once these are understood, project management can be fit into the appropriate context and sold more proactively.

Response

Sellers need to move away from selling project management by focusing on specific features, and learn to reframe the information in terms of benefits and the benefits' connection to values relative to the executive's priorities. One way of doing this is by drawing analogies about the impact project failures have on the business strategy and discussing lessons learned. The goal is to stimulate deep learning on both sides, as opposed to making uninformed associations about the negative value of project management based on a fear of repeating past mistakes.

Proof

It helps to provide anecdotal information or proof of the value proposition in a context that senior executives will relate to, e.g., restate the value of project management in terms that support the business objective and corporate strategies. This requires a focused response that is adaptable to changing contextual factors and that reflects clear alignment between business goals and project management.

Project management is a tough sell in a competitive environment characterized by a lack of boundaries and innovative partnering strategies. Credibility and trust are important advantages to have and they contribute to successful services selling.

Why Is It Difficult to Sell Project Management to Senior Executives?

Although project management is perceived to have value in areas of improving operational efficiency and contributing to a firm's competitive advantage, the perceptions of its organizational benefits are not always aligned between the senior executives who may buy or invest in the services, the practitioners who apply the discipline, and the consultants who are involved in selling it. Senior executives focus on business goals, results, and outcomes from projects, while practitioners and consultants tend to focus on the tactics of tools and techniques. Overall, there is a general lack of awareness of the value of project management to help businesses shift trajectories in anticipation of market changes. The emphasis on different values of project management, that the other party may not support, lends credence to earlier works (Delisle 2001; Thomas 2000) that suggests that this trap is riddled with substantial language barriers and considerable difficulty in developing a shared understanding and appreciation of the internal and external goals that project management could help businesses achieve.

Like marketing personnel, project managers need to be skillful at selling the benefits of project management to the senior executives by relating the benefits of project management to performance measures defined as critical by senior management. These measures relate to:

- Values in efficiency (e.g., return on investment, cost reductions, revenue generation, and increased market share)
- Values in effectiveness (e.g., organizational effectiveness and customer satisfaction)
- Values in market expansion/innovation (EIU 1999).

Because of the lack of understanding about value and project management, difficulty exists in gaining appropriate management attention to present convincing reasons to senior executives about why and how their organizations will benefit from the use of project management. Hence, long-term investment in project management remains a tough sell at the senior executive level.

Conclusion of Phase I Findings

Our findings suggest that significant disconnects exist between what sellers promote and what buyers want to hear regarding project management. Senior executives fail to see project management's connection with the goals of the organization. In addition, the sale of project management, at present, appears to be the response to internal crises or changes in the environment that may be triggered by issues, activities, people, and such, that are vulnerable and susceptible to being triggered, instead of occurring as a proactive business decision.

To summarize, Phase I of our research found that:

- Project management is sold from a foundation values perspective and has not evolved toward the full consideration of innovation values (as described in Chapter 2).

- There are a number of disconnects that relate to the understanding of project management and its perceived value in business terms. More work is needed to create the awareness in practitioners of project management's true potential and value at a strategic level.

- Sellers of project management (including project managers) need to use effective marketing strategies and communication skills in presenting project management to senior executives in a business context, not only a project or operational context.

- Sellers need to be mindful of the dynamics around change management and ensure that they adjust their sales strategies accordingly. Company cultures are ingrained and change can be painfully slow. Recommending small-scale project management initiatives and "quick-win" strategies will go farther than changes that are more dramatic. However, these initiatives must be closely tied to strategic business results and not simply efficiency initiatives.

- Worldwide, organizations are evolving in terms of project management maturity (Cabanis 1998; CCTA 2000; CIPPM 2001; Compass 2001; Cooke-Davies 2000; Dinsmore 1998; ESI-International 2001; Hartman and Skulmoski 1998; Ibbs and Kwak 1997; 1998; 2000; IPMA 2000; Kerzner 2001). This statement relates to the 2 x 2 matrices presented in this chapter that depict levels of maturity of organizations in terms of the buyer-seller relationship from Quadrant 1 to Quadrant 4. Sellers need to be aware of this range as they develop their strategies to promote and sell project management.[3]

- Effective relationships between buyers and sellers, built on trust and past experiences with each other, are critical to future working relationships and potential sales (Lesser 2000). These relationships cannot be built over the course of a few meetings. Sellers need to ensure that they cultivate these relationships and develop their credibility with senior executives.

The findings from Phase I reveal common trends or relationships that warrant further research and elaboration. Positioning (how to sell) and branding (creating positive awareness) of project management appear to be central issues in establishing project management as a strategic capability. Both areas warrant further research, with respect to their relationship in the complex topic of selling project management.

Summary

To summarize, this chapter addressed the question, "Why is it difficult to sell project management to senior executives?" The chapter looked at participant understanding of project management and identified any gaps that may exist in understanding value and selling/buying project management. Then it looked at the process of selling project management and the interaction patterns between the buyer and seller. The chapter developed several models to explain the process of selling project management and the challenges involved. It also developed a model on the common decision processes involved in buying project management. Based on these findings and the literature review, we next compiled a survey instrument to generalize and explore these issues on a wider scale. The next chapter elaborates on the Phase II results.

Notes

1. These results were initially presented to the *PMI Research Conference 2000* in Paris, France in June 2000 and, subsequently, a paper was published as an article in the *Project Management Journal*® (June 2002) and as a chapter in *The Frontiers of Project Management Research*, co-edited by, Denis P. Slevin, David Cleland, and Jeffrey Pinto (PMI 2002). This chapter represents a major revision of that earlier paper although some parts may be identical and are reproduced with permission of PMI.

2. This principle from economic theory has been widely validated in contingent valuation studies.

3. Tying the work on project management maturity levels to issues of selling project management is beyond the scope of this study, but is an important area that deserves further study.

CHAPTER 5

Phase II Findings: Demographics and Practices

This chapter presents high-level findings from the second phase of the research project. The primary research question for this phase of the study was, "How do you sell project management to senior executives?" In order to answer this question we collected a large database of information on the status of project management practice in organizations today, and the success of those attempting to sell project management to senior executives. The information was collected with the web-based instrument described in Chapter 3. This chapter provides the demographics of our respondents and the reported practices of project management by respondent group, industry, and country. We also report on the status of project management practice in today's organizations and the gaps between expectations and outcomes.

Survey Respondents

In examining the demographics of respondents, we looked at three categories. First, we reviewed the general respondent characteristics and then looked at project management characteristics. Finally, we examined the organizational characteristics. In general, the participants represent a diverse group of respondents, who reflect the varied nature of organizations and individuals involved in project management in organizations today. In total 1,867 individuals responded to the survey. The survey has an accuracy rate of +/- 2.27 percent, 19 times out of 20.

Next is a brief description of these respondents.

General Respondent Demographics

Study participants comprise a well-educated, experienced, and mobile group, representative of the sample population. Some highlights on individual characteristics are as follows:

- More than one-half broadly identify their role within their organization as project personnel (53 percent), 26 percent as a consultant, and 20 percent as a senior executive.

- Seventy percent of participants are male and 71 percent are between the ages of 31 and 50. Sixty-three percent are over 40.

- Three-quarters report possessing at least one university undergraduate degree.

- The majority of participants live in either the United States (55 percent) or Canada (35 percent).

- Nearly six-in-ten participants (57 percent) have been with their current employer for 5 years or less, and 42 percent work for companies that employ 1,000 or fewer individuals.

- Participants range in their responsibility levels from being project team members to those managing program portfolios or sponsoring projects.

Project Management Demographics

On average, survey respondents have significant levels of engagement with the project management profession, as indicated by their level of project management experience and level of project responsibility. Additionally, over 50 percent belong to project management professional associations. At the same time, slightly more than 50 percent have taken no more than single, short project management training courses. Further specifics follow:

- Fifty-three percent of respondents belong to a professional project management organization, while 19 percent possess a professional project management designation.

- Nearly six-in-ten participants (58 percent) have ten years or less project management experience. The greatest proportion of respondents consider their firm's primary business activity to be either consulting or information technology (17 percent and 16 percent, respectively). Within their organizations, most work either in the information technology/computers/software area (40 percent) or in project management (30 percent).

- The highest level of project responsibility attained by the greatest proportion of respondents is either a project manager (39 percent) or a program manager (32 percent).

- Six-in-ten (59 percent) spend the majority of their time on project management-related activities during an average week. Sixty-three percent expect that it is likely that the amount of time they spend on project management will increase in the future.

- The majority of participants (54 percent) have taken no more than individual project management courses. Similar proportions have a Project Management Professional (PMP®) certification or equivalent certification, or have a project management education certificate (18 percent and 14 percent, respectively).

Organizational Characteristics

The survey respondents come from a wide variety of organizations in many industries and of disparate sizes. In general, most of the respondents come from functional areas within their organization, where project management would be expected to be an important issue (information technology or project management). The industry distribution is a wide and varied selection of industries reflecting the increased projectized nature of organizations today. Respondents are almost evenly spread across small and large organizations. Specifics follow:

- Seventy percent of respondents worked within the information technology or project management areas of their organization.

- Approximately 50 percent of the respondents came from organizations whose main business activity falls in the following six industries: consulting, information technology, telecommunications, government, manufacturing, or engineering/construction.

- While 30 percent of all firms had gross sales of less than $50 million (USD) during the calendar year 2000, a nearly equal number had sales of $1 billion dollars or more.

- Roughly, one-third of the organizations represented had less than 1,000 employees (26 percent) and one-third (30 percent) had over 10,000 employees.

Status of Project Management

Survey results strongly supported the qualitative model presented in Figure 4.2, where a trigger that may exist as a vulnerable area internally or externally may ignite a crisis in the organization. Senior executives then go through steps of problem recognition, seeking information (internally or externally), and either not acting (results in the accidental project manager) or acting in one of two ways. Tactical actions are quick fixes, such as making verbal changes but not taking real action, for example, buying software to manage projects and other such actions. Strategic actions are longer-term, business-driven actions that include hiring new project managers, investing in staff training and education, and so on. These are developed in the first phase of the project. In particular, the following descriptive statistics provide support for the model.

- 71.1 percent agreed that the selling issue is an important one for their organization (slightly—33.4 percent; strongly—37.7 percent).

- Forty-five percent agreed (12.4 percent of this total strongly agreed) that selling project management was difficult to do within their organizations. At the same time, 39.5 percent disagreed (11.3 percent of this total strongly disagreed) with this statement.

- 21.8 percent of our respondents strongly agree with the statement that project management is a valued discipline in organizations, ranking with accounting, finance, and engineering. At the same time, 11.8 percent strongly disagree.

- Approximately 60 percent of respondents believe that senior management understands the cost of unsuccessful projects, but only 20 percent agree that their senior management provides meaningful support for project management initiatives.

- The concept of the "accidental project manager" is well supported in this survey. 60.2 percent of respondents agree that the title of project manager is usually not accompanied by increased pay or recognition, while 57.8 percent agree that little or no project management training is given to those who take on the role of project manager. Fewer than 60 percent report that project managers receive little or no formal training, while 51 percent believe that project managers do not "have the authority to do what is needed to manage projects properly."

- 58.6 percent agreed that project management is used in times of crises, and 16.7 percent of respondents strongly agreed that this was the case.

Value of Project Management in Today's Organizations

In collecting data on how to sell project management, we captured interesting insights into the value placed on project management in today's organizations. Some of these insights are provided in the following list.

- A large proportion of participants (82 percent) agree that project management is used to increase the likelihood of delivering successful projects.

- While 60 percent agree, "projects are usually aligned with my company's strategic plans," 60 percent disagree that projects within their company are usually completed on schedule or on budget.

- More than seven-in-ten agree that project management enhances customer satisfaction (73 percent) and their firm's performance in non-financial ways (71 percent).

- Just over 70 percent of respondents strongly agree that project management enhances customer satisfaction.

These descriptions of project management support its increasing importance in today's organizations. The majority of respondents recognized project management as having strategic, as well as tactical, value in their organization. At the same time, there remains between 20 and 30 percent of respondents who do not recognize project management as having a strategic role to play.

Further breakdowns of the characteristics of those holding these differing perceptions will be conducted in future studies to determine if these perceptions are distributed across industries, levels in organizations, and countries. This analysis will make an important contribution to our understanding of project management's value in today's organizations.

Key Questions to Highlight

In order to highlight some of the key results with respect to the status of project management in organizations today, we chose eleven questions to examine in more detail. The eleven questions, with results for the entire sample, are depicted in Table 5.1.

The first two questions in Table 5.1 explored the use of project management practices in organizations. For the sample as a whole, only 39 percent agree with the statement that appropriate project management tools, techniques, and methodologies are used in their organization. At the same time, 43 percent of respondents agree that interactions among projects are

Table 5.1. Status of Project Management

Question	Status of Project Management	Net Agree%*	Net Disagree%
1	Appropriate project management tools, techniques, methodologies are used	39	48
2	Interactions among projects are managed	43	44
3	Projects consistently come in on time, on budget	25	60
4	Projects consistently meet specifications	39	47
5	Projects are usually aligned with strategic plans	60	24
6	Project managers have little or no formal training	58	31
7	Adequate funding to support project management	44	41
8	Realistic expectations of project management	49	35
9	There is resistance to project management	37	44
10	Project management is a valued discipline	48	38
11	Project management is used in times of crisis	48	37

* The net percentage is based on percentage of "strongly agree" and "agree" only and "strongly disagree" and "disagree" only, and does not include "neither agree nor disagree." Thus, the total of agree and disagree across columns does not equal 100 percent.

appropriately managed. This data suggests that the many respondents believe that their organizations are using what few methods they may have well enough to manage interactions among projects. This belief points to the underlying attitude of "doing business the same way because it seems to work, and thus, there is no need to invest in more or different project management options."

The next three questions in Table 5.1 explore the respondent's perceptions around project outcomes. Only 25 percent of respondents agree that projects consistently come in on time and on budget. The results also show that 39 percent of respondents agree that projects consistently meet specifications. This outcome speaks to the multidimensional aspect of project success, particularly that meeting specifications may not be tightly linked to meeting the schedule. As discussed in Chapter 2, studies in the literature have shown that the budget and schedule explain a relatively small portion of variance in explaining project success. In particular, Delisle's (2001) factor analysis shows a high factor loading for the success criteria "meeting technical specifications and meeting operational specifications," which accounts for just under 20 percent of the variance or power in explaining which success criteria are considered most critical in judging the success of a project.

Meanwhile, respondents report a high level of agreement (60 percent) with the statement that projects are usually aligned with strategic plans. This data, in conjunction with the previous data, seems to indicate that the organization has a large number of projects that are aligned with strategic plans, but only sometimes meet specification objectives, and rarely do so within the expected budget and timeline. As well, the perceptions that respondents have may not reflect what is actually happening and, thus, the triggers that have the potential to ignite crises are not really paid the attention they deserve.

The next question in Table 5.1 provides support for the accidental project manager concept. A majority (58 percent) of the respondents agree with the statement that project managers in their organization receive little or no formal project management training. This finding clearly validates the findings and interpretations from Phase I concerning the prevalence of accidental project managers in today's organizations.

Finally, the last five questions explore senior executive support for project management in their organizations. Forty-four percent of respondents believe that senior executives provide appropriate funding to support project management in their organizations, and 49 percent of senior executives have realistic expectations of project management. However, 37 percent of respondents report resistance to implementing project management in their organization.

This result is interesting since almost half agree that project management is a valued discipline, like finance and accounting, in their organization. Clearly, the understanding of value and expectations to deliver value, as described in Chapter 2, needs to be examined by sellers and buyers. Evidence of a difference in understanding value is that almost half of the respondents agree that project management is used in times of crises in their organization. Thus, value may be more tied to tactical fixes, in reality, even though respondents report that project management is a valued discipline and not just a tool or technique.

These results suggest a couple of interesting conundrums. First, if senior executives seem to have realistic expectations of project management, why are organizations unable to deliver on projects? Second, approximately one-half of the sample reports adequate funding and many respondents report highly valuing the practice of project management, so again, why are organizations continuing to struggle to meet project objectives and gain senior executive support?

In order to explore these issues further, we report on these same questions, breaking the responses out into demographic sub-samples based on position of respondent, country of origin, and industry. These breakdowns provide some further interesting insights.

Breakdown by Position

Table 5.2 reports the responses of project management personnel, consultants, and senior executives. Project management personnel responses are shown in the first column, consultants are in the second, and senior executives in the third column. Project management personnel includes staff positions ranging from team members up to program directors, but the majority of the sample are project managers or higher. Consultants are those who sell project management for a living. Senior executives are executives at the vice president level or higher, who are responsible for projects in their organizations.

This section highlights the different perceptions (supported statistically) held by senior executives. The sample, as a whole, shows that senior executives are less likely to believe that projects are aligned with strategic plans than project personnel are, and consultants are even less likely to believe that projects are strategic. This finding could reflect a number of things: a need of project personnel to believe their work is strategically important; an objective outside opinion of the consultant; a consultant perception based on the level of senior executive support for the projects they work on in organizations; a senior executive belief that projects are operational and tactical, not strategic. Regardless of the cause of these differences, the existence of the difference in this magnitude is sure to cause conflicts in priorities and difficulties on projects.

Another interesting anomaly in the findings relates to the high level of agreement between senior executives and consultants on the measure of accidental project managers. Both are significantly higher than the project personnel. This difference could reflect a lack of awareness on the part of these groups of available training services, training needs, and the level of development of the project managers. Alternately, internally promoted staff may take on the new position for other reasons, which may relate to perceived status and control, and be reluctant to admit that they are not well prepared to manage projects. Regardless of the exact reasons, this discrepancy should be a flag of potential problems.

Finally, and perhaps not surprisingly, senior executives believe that their expectations of project management are realistic—significantly more often than do project personnel and consultants. This result, again, is a clear indicator of a cognitive gap between these groups, which is sure to cause significant problems for those managing projects on the front lines. The results of these questions by country are equally interesting, as depicted in Table 5.3.

Breakdown by Country

Two points of interest come up in the comparisons in Table 5.3. First, Canada and the United States have a similar outlook on the status of project management on all of these questions. Second, the rest of the world seems to be doing slightly

Table 5.2. Status of Project Management by Position

Question	Status of Project Management	Project Personnel 997	Consultants 489	Senior Executives 381	Total 1,867
		Percent Net Agree (%)			
1	Appropriate project management tools, techniques, methodologies are used	41	33	40	39
2	Interactions among projects are managed	44	35	52	43
3	Projects consistently come in on time, on budget	25	22	29	25
4	Projects consistently meet specifications	40	33	44	39
5	Projects are usually aligned with strategic plans	60	24	46	60
6	Project managers have little or no formal training	55	62	61	58
7	Adequate funding to support project management	48	36	47	44
8	Realistic expectations of project management	48	41	59	49
9	There is resistance to project management	35	47	30	37
10	Project management is a valued discipline	51	37	53	48
11	Project management is used in times of crisis	43	58	49	48

better than either Canada or the United States on many of these measures, particularly around project outcomes, project management funding, and the use of tools. At the same time, the rest of the world does poorer on some key measures, such as experiencing resistance to project management, aligning to strategic plans, and meeting project specifications. These differences suggest the need for more cross-cultural research into the application of project management globally. The difference in investment patterns might be a concern for North American-based project management organizations, as it may indicate that in a globally competitive business environment, funding levels should be carefully monitored to allow for strategic investment in project management.

However, there are a few key limitations to take into consideration in understanding these results. First, the rest of the world represents a small part of the sample in comparison to Canadian and United States participants, and thus, the rest of world statistics may not be representative of any one country, or all countries. Second, the respondents from the rest of the world may not have as easily accessible technology to complete the Internet-based survey. In addition, the respondents from the rest of the world may have been particularly interested in project management research because of the investment their companies were making in it.

Breakdown by Industry

Examining these same questions by industry also highlights some interesting trends in the data. These results are presented in Table 5.4.

The dark gray highlighting in Table 5.4 helps to illuminate the industry with the highest percentage for each question. Similarly, the light gray squares highlight the lowest percentages for each statement.

Table 5.3. Status of Project Management by Country*

Question	Status of Project Management	Canada 638	United States 1,021	Rest of World 208	Total 1,867
		Percent Net Agree (%)			
1	Appropriate project management tools, techniques, methodologies are used	40	38	51	39
2	Interactions among projects are managed	44	42	48	43
3	Projects consistently come in on time, on budget	28	22	38	25
4	Projects consistently meet specifications	42	37	32	39
5	Projects are usually aligned with strategic plans	62	59	41	60
6	Project managers have little or no formal training	58	57	48	58
7	Adequate funding to support project management	41	46	56	44
8	Realistic expectations of project management	49	48	41	49
9	There is resistance to project management	32	40	60	37
10	Project management is a valued discipline	49	47	49	48
11	Project management is used in times of crisis	46	49	54	48

* The total column on the far right of the table represents the average response for the entire sample, thus, by calculating straight averages, the percentage totals are not the same. To calculate the values in the last column of the table, take the number of respondents, multiply by the percent for each group, as follows: (638 x 40%) (Canada) + (1,021x 38%) (USA) + (208 x 51%) (Rest of the World) = 39%.

Many trends appear in the data—we comment on a few of the most noteworthy, with respect to the interpretations of the study research questions. First, participants from the Telecom industry report the highest level of agreement that the appropriate project management tools are being used, projects are strategically aligned, projects consistently meet specifications, and appropriate levels of funding are provided. These organizations also report the lowest levels of resistance to project management and fewer project managers with little or no formal training. These results may point to the type of organizational structure used in the industry. The Telecom industry is highly projectized, where most work is carried out as projects. The recognition of the strategic importance of these projects is high and clearly understood by the industry as a whole. Respondents from this industry believe that project management is appropriately supported in their organizations.[1]

Second, Table 5.3 presents some surprising results from the consulting industry. We asked participants to respond to these questions based on what they observed in their own organization. We later asked which industry their organization belonged to. Thus, we infer that this category refers to consultant's judgments of the status of project management within consulting organizations. This industry has the lowest level of support for statements that project interactions are managed, projects are strategically aligned, and project management is recognized as an important discipline and appropriately funded. This outcome seems atypical given that consulting is an industry where a considerable amount of the work may be considered as projects. It could be an indication of a work environment where profit margins and revenue incentives

Table 5.4. Status of Project Management by Industry

Question	Status of Project Management	Consulting 309	Information Technology 289	Government 167	Telecom 113	Manufacturing & Processing 96	Construction & Engineering 71	Total 1,868*
		Net Percent Agree (%)						
1	Appropriate project management tools, techniques, methodologies are used	35	38	31	57	39	43	39
2	Interactions among projects are managed	37	46	40	55	47	56	43
3	Projects consistently come in on time, on budget	23	26	19	34	21	46	25
4	Projects consistently meet specifications	35	41	29	53	44	52	39
5	Projects are usually aligned with strategic plans	49	49	55	68	62	64	60
6	Project managers have little or no formal training	63	51	59	48	61	66	58
7	Adequate funding to support project management	35	46	38	53	41	51	44
8	Realistic expectations of project management	45	45	43	59	49	56	49
9	There is resistance to project management	44	34	41	21	27	26	37
10	Project management is a valued discipline	37	57	47	60	48	59	48
11	Project management is used in times of crisis	56	57	45	55	36	50	48

* Note that the industries represented above are the six most represented in our sample. The average response is again for the entire sample. Thus, the industry averages reported above do not average to the total figure.

drive the acceptance, management, and alignment of projects more than project management. Just because an organization is projectized does not necessarily mean that that organization's members are practicing "good" project management. Also, this category reported quite a high level of agreement (nearly 60 percent) that project management is used in times of crises. This data further supports that notion that knowing does not often translate into doing, especially by those selling the merits of project management.

At the same time, one industry you would expect to perform well in project management—construction and engineering—does report consistent results as anticipated. Respondents report the highest support for how their organizations manage project interactions and outcomes, with respect to cost and schedule. However, they also report the highest level of agreement for the statement that project managers have little or no formal project management training. This makes

Table 5.5. Knowing-Doing Gaps

Knowing	Doing	Results
39% applying appropriate project management methods	44% report adequate funding to support project management	25% of projects consistently come in on budget or schedule
48% recognize project management as valued discipline	58% report little formal project management training	39% of projects meet specifications
49% believe that senior executive expectations are realistic	69% spend over 50% of time on project management	60% of projects are aligned with strategic objectives

sense given the nature of the business and the length of time project management has been practiced in this industry. Typically, construction and engineering people have engineering management training, both in the classroom and on the job. But, it does not seem that they connect that to project management training. Although the issue does not appear to be caused by resisting change, it may be related to not having the time to learn new tools and techniques, being intimidated, or not being motivated to invest in learning new tools when around half of projects are already meeting time, cost, and specification expectations.

Government seems to have the most dismal record in many respects. The results show that less than 20 percent of respondents agree that projects come in on time and on budget, and less than 30 percent believe that they are meeting specifications. Not using the appropriate project management tools and techniques, combined with not being adequately funded, leaves a lot of room for improvement in this sector. It should be noted that government is not traditionally as projectized as the other industries in our top six respondents, and project management has come relatively recently to this sector (with the exception, of course, of the large scale military and National Aeronautics and Space Administration establishments). These results could, thus, reflect their position on the project management learning curve. They could also be indicative of the way these projects are being completed (often extensive use of contractors) and the types of contracts involved (often cost plus). Clearly future research here is warranted given the large number of projects undertaken by governments.

The information technology (IT) sector seems to follow many of these trends, albeit, respondents report less resistance in the organization and a higher value of project management. Perhaps the most interesting finding is the high reported agreement on the use of project management (nearly 70 percent) in times of crises. This percentage speaks to the need for the IT industry to examine decisions to invest in project management, since only around half of projects are reported to be aligned at the strategic level. Thus, senior executives who set high expectations should not be too surprised if the outcomes do not meet these expectations.

Conclusions

The concept of the knowing-doing gap was introduced earlier in this document. This chapter illustrates the knowing-doing gap in project management implementation, as empirically reported in a sample of 1,867 project personnel, consultants, and senior executives. Table 5.5 summarizes the findings with respect to the status of project management in today's organizations, as depicted by the entire respondent sample.

On the knowing side, these statistics show that, while only 39 percent of the sample believes that appropriate project management methods are being used in their organizations, most believe that there is something that can be described as "appropriate methods," which are not being applied. Alternately, they might not define and report what they are doing as a project management method. Whatever the case, the investment in project management has thus far not had as great an impact as needed, compared to the effort that companies that make the tools and techniques of project management, which many consider appropriate, are spending on espousing their benefits.

In addition, just fewer than 50 percent of respondents believe that project management is recognized as a valued discipline in their organizations. This percentage provides evidence of the increasing importance of projects in today's economy. Finally, 49 percent believe that senior executive's expectations of project management are realistic.

On the doing side, only 44 percent report that senior management provides adequate funding to support project management, and 58 percent report that project managers in their organizations have little or no formal project management training, while the demographic data reported earlier shows that 69 percent of the respondents report spending over 50 percent of their time on project management, and expect it to increase in the future. Here we see indications that project management is indeed becoming increasingly important and present in today's organizations in terms of the time spent on it. At the same time, senior executive support for project management is lower and the majority of project managers receive little or no formal training.

Finally, the study's statistics show that we have strategically important projects that are not meeting specification, cost, or schedule expectations consistently. It appears we have accidental project managers managing strategically important projects that are not achieving the outcomes they expect, and they are not using the appropriate project management tools and techniques. The results suggest that, while organizations believe that there are such things as appropriate methods (that is, they know how to manage projects), they are woefully inept in doing it effectively. Either project management expectations are realistic and there is something wrong with our implementation of project management in a majority of organizations, or expectations are inconsistent with the types of outcomes necessary for organizational success. It is time to determine which it is.

Summary

This chapter presents the simple descriptive findings from this large-scale survey exploring the practice of project management in today's organizations. In doing so, these results and interpretations make a significant addition to our empirical knowledge base about the emerging profession of project management.

However, further, more sophisticated analysis of this dataset is necessary to completely address the issues of how to sell project management to senior executives. The next chapter presents the findings of the analysis that answers this question by examining the gaps between the arguments and processes used by very successful and very unsuccessful project managers and consultants, and comparing these to the arguments senior executives identify as successful. Chapter 6 also draws on exploratory factor analysis and theory developed around strategic issue identification from Chapter 2 and Chapter 4, to allow us to draw conclusions about how to best sell project management to senior executives.

Notes

1. The results should be interpreted with caution since this data was collected in the first quarter of 2001, before the Telecom industry was severely impacted by a decreased demand for its products. These results could be very different if the study were conducted today.

CHAPTER 6

Phase II Findings: How Do You Sell Project Management to Senior Executives?

Chapter 6 presents the data analysis related to answering the question, "How do you sell project management to senior executives?" As mentioned in Chapter 1, the concept of selling is defined as promoting and advocating project management to senior executives in an organized manner. The first part of this chapter presents a brief summary of the key descriptive statistics pertaining to how to sell project management to senior executives. The majority of this chapter presents the organization of the data models, key findings revealed by the models, and synthesis of the findings of the final iterations of the Exploratory Factor Analysis (EFA) of Phase II data. These models provide the basis for interpretation of results concerning the interrelationships between the selling context, processes, and arguments pertaining to how to sell project management to senior executives.

Descriptive Summary

Although slightly more than seven-in-ten (71 percent) survey participants agreed that selling project management to senior executives is an important issue in their organizations, many sellers (45 percent) expressed difficulty in selling project management at this level. The following descriptive statements help summarize the important responses to the questions asked on the survey pertaining to respondents' experiences with selling project management. The percentages in this section are the "net agree," which combines both strongly agree and agree. The full data tables are provided in Appendix C.

- Two-thirds (67 percent) of respondents agree that project management is more effectively sold to senior executives when project managers are involved in the process (Table 6, Appendix C).

- Three-quarters or more of participants agree that senior executives are more interested in project management when "there is an internal project crisis or failure" (77 percent), or when "they hear about earlier project successes at their company" (75 percent) (Table 7, Appendix C).

- Nearly eight-in-ten (79 percent) respondents agree that when selling project management to senior executives, it is helpful if the senior executives are supportive and approachable, or when the seller is seen as credible (Table 6, Appendix C).

- Eighty-five percent agree that presenting project management as a "technique to help achieve the company mission or [to] reach a specific project goal" is helpful in selling project management to senior executives (Table 9, Appendix C).

- A large proportion of respondents (87 percent) *agree* that using "simple, clear language" is helpful when selling project management to senior executives.

- Eighty-five percent of respondents agree that linking project management to corporate goals and business objectives is an effective strategy in selling project management to senior executives.

Table 6.1. Model Names and Relationship to Groups

Model #	Model Name	Sample Size[*]	Included Group(s)
1	GENERAL SELLING BASE MODEL	n = 743	All project managers and consultants
2	PROJECT PERSONNEL SELLING MODEL	n = 499	Project personnel only
3	CONSULTANT SELLING MODEL	n = 244	Consultants only
4	VERY SUCCESSFUL SELLING BASE MODEL	n = 99	Project personnel and consultants
5	VERY SUCCESSFUL PROJECT PERSONNEL MODEL	n = 61	Project personnel who were very successful in selling only
6	VERY SUCCESSFUL CONSULTANT MODEL	n = 38	Consultants who were very successful in selling only
7	VERY UNSUCCESSFUL SELLING MODEL	n = 19	All project managers and consultants
8	SENIOR EXECUTIVE MODEL	n = 190	Senior executives only

* These sample sizes are one-half the size of the total sample. This analysis is conducted on one-half of the data to retain a matched half for future testing purposes.

- At the same time, a notable portion of participants *disagree* that emphasizing "detailed features, tools, or techniques" (30 percent) or using "emotional, dramatic, or novel terms"(43 percent) are helpful ways of describing project management when selling to senior executives (Table 10, Appendix C).

This reflects the data's ability to identify both successful and unsuccessful selling practices.

These findings largely support the model derived from the Phase I study. However, they do not, in themselves, reveal some of the important conditions under which project management is successfully sold in organizations. To reveal those arguments and processes that are most successful in selling project management to senior executives, we conducted an iterative EFA (described in detail in the methodology section). The analysis of this data provides insight into the key successful arguments and processes in use today, and how these arguments relate to the selling context or environment.

Summary of Process Steps to Produce Models

As described in Chapter 3, the EFA process essentially boils the survey questions down into groups or "sets of factors" that point to the key selling processes and arguments in selling project management to senior executives.

The next step was to reveal underlying combinations or patterns of the concepts (independent variables) that have the greatest explanatory power. In research terms, this refers to those factors that explain the highest percentage of the overall variance.

As explained in Chapter 3, we applied Principal Component Analysis (PCA) to this factor analysis data to transform this set of factors into "composites" or models (Cooper and Emory 1995). The models show the relationship among concepts, although they cannot show that one independent variable causes the other to increase or decrease. Thus, the interpretations of the data cannot comment on the need for "more" or "less" of each type of argument or process in selling.

As well, these processes allowed us to determine if there were differences between the arguments and processes used by those describing themselves as *successful* and *unsuccessful* in selling project management and, finally, to make comparisons between very successful and unsuccessful models. The eight data models represent the culmination of progressive iterations of the data using increasingly stringent cut-off limits, as discussed in Chapter 3. The eight models presented in Chapter 4 are reproduced here in Table 6.1 for quick reference in going through this very dense set of results/interpretations. The models in Table 6.1 are presented in the order in which they were developed to help the reader follow the description of the process of how the models were developed. The model "labels" are shown in capital letters in the text to help the reader easily find them in the text

The first goal was to explore how project management is typically sold in organizations. To do this, we needed to determine the key arguments and processes, regardless of whether the seller was unsuccessful or successful. Thus, model one, the GENERAL SELLING BASE MODEL, reflects all project personnel and consultants, regardless of the level of success they reported.

We further refined the GENERAL SELLING BASE MODEL to explore whether project personnel and consultants use similar or different approaches to selling project management. The next two models split up the groups to allow for cross-group comparisons. These models are called the PROJECT PERSONNEL SELLING MODEL and the CONSULTANT SELLING MODEL, respectively.

Next, the exploration shifted to finding out how project management is successfully sold to senior executives by looking at the context, arguments, and processes of respondents who report being very successful in selling project management to senior executives. Analysis of this data led to the development of the VERY SUCCESSFUL SELLING BASE MODEL. This base model combined project personnel and consultants. We then examined the differences between the groups (project personnel and consultants), which resulted in two new models, the VERY SUCCESSFUL PROJECT PERSONNEL MODEL and the VERY SUCCESSFUL CONSULTANT MODEL.

The next model represents the very unsuccessful sellers as a group. The resulting model was called the VERY UNSUCCESSFUL SELLING MODEL. Comparing this model to the very successful selling models allows us to differentiate between what the successful people are doing differently than others.

Finally, we use the data from the comparative analysis from senior executives to develop the SENIOR EXECUTIVE MODEL.

The following sections synthesize the findings and insights from the development of the eight models listed in Table 6.1. The first section looks at the general findings from the sample as a whole, and then breaks it down into project personnel and consultants to explore any differences in how they approach the selling task. This comparative analysis allows us to explore the hypothesis that project personnel and consultants use different approaches to selling project management. The next section looks at the data from those project personnel and consultants reporting very successful or very unsuccessful sales of project management to senior executives. This analysis allows us to explore whether there are significant differences in selling approaches and arguments between those reporting high levels of success in selling project management to senior executives and those reporting being very unsuccessful. The third section looks at the data collected from senior executives to provide insights into what convinces senior executives to invest in project management. The next section provides a comparison of the eight models. The chapter concludes by identifying best practices and key considerations as derived from this data analysis.

How Do We Generally Attempt to Sell Project Management to Senior Executives?

This section explores how attempts are made to sell project management to senior executives, in general, across the sample. The discussion provides a general picture of the main arguments, processes, and context within which project management is sold to senior executives.

GENERAL SELLING BASE MODEL (n = 743)

In the GENERAL SELLING BASE MODEL, ten factors were identified to explain how to sell project management to senior executives. However, only nine are statistically significant (the eighth factor was not significant). Because the data analysis does not actually assign a name or descriptive "label" to each factor, we labeled each one, attempting to convey the appropriate meaning. These nine factors, identified in the far left column of Table 6.2, are shown in order of importance, including: Executive Framing (most important), Alignment, Value Statements, Iron Triangle, Project Management Salespeople, Competition, Accidental Project Manager, External Consultants, and Crisis (least important). The nine significant factors in the GENERAL SELLING BASE MODEL, as a whole, account for 56.2 percent of the variance, and the top three factors

Table 6.2. Exploratory Factor Analysis for the General Selling Base Model

Factor	Items	Items from Survey
1 Executive Framing	9_1	Successful approach—discuss how project management fits company's business
	10_1	Frame project management as having a high payoff with few negative consequences
	10_2	Frame project management as an executive decision
	10_3	Present project management as a solution to a specific problem
	10_4	Frame project management as uncovering issues, identifying solutions
	10_5	Frame project management as technique to achieve company mission or goals
	11_1	Describe project management with simple, clear language
	11_3	Describe project management with positive words (success, savings)
	11_4	Describe project management as contributing to firm's long term benefits
	11_5	Describe project management using senior executive language
	11_7	Describe project management using supporting evidence, facts to justify value
	12_1	Use informal communication practices, e.g., discuss in hallways
	12_3	Link project management to corporate goals, business objectives
	12_4	Describe project management's value as fixing a specific "point of pain"
2 Alignment	2_4	Senior management approves adequate funding for project management
	2_5	Senior management's expectations are realistic
	2_6	Senior management expectations are attainable
	2_7	Senior management understands that project management is investment in long-term firm success
	3_1	Project management is aligned with company's operational/business goals
	3_2	Project management is aligned with company's strategic goals
	3_6	Decision-makers consider cross project interactions
	4_5	Projects are aligned with company's strategic plans
3 Value Statements	6_1	Project management contributes to improved financial measures
	6_2	Project management enhances staff growth and development
	6_3	Project management enhances customer satisfaction, profits, market share
	6_5	Project management helps firm compete better than competition
	6_6	Project management enhances firm's non-financial performance
4 Iron Triangle	4_1	Projects are managed with appropriate tools, techniques, methodologies
	4_2	Projects at firm are completed on schedule
	4_3	Projects at firm are completed on budget
	4_4	Projects at firm are completed within objectives (scope)
5 Project Management Salespeople	7_2	Effective selling of project management involves PMO staff
	7_3	Effective selling of project management involves project management staff
6 Competition	8_1	Executive interested in project management when the competition is doing better
	8_2	Senior executives interested in project management when they see new business opportunities
7 Accidental Project Manager	5_1	Project managers have little or no formal training in the discipline
	5_2	People are assigned project management titles without promotions or pay increases
8		NOT SIGNIFICANT
9 External Consultants	7_4	Effective selling involves external marketing/sales staff
	7_5	Effective selling involves external consultants
10 Crisis	3_4	Project management is used in times of crises
	8_3	There is an internal project crisis or failure

(Executive Framing, Alignment, and Value Statements), as a whole, account for 34.4 percent of the variance.

The actual questions that formed these factors are called "items" in Table 6.2, with the item number in the middle column, and the actual items listed in the last or far right column of the table. These items are the questions in the online survey, used in Phase II, which provided the data we used to conduct the EFA and build each specific model.

In Table 6.2, the dark gray highlight indicates the specific item that had the highest score, or in research terms "loading," to help explain factors in the GENERAL SELLING BASE MODEL. Scores represent the strongest correlation, or greatest ability of the item to explain a particular factor of the ten listed in Table 6.2. For example, item 11_3 refers to the actual question in the survey instrument. The item asked respondents about the extent to which they agree with the statement that "describing project management using positive words such as success, opportunity, or savings made it easier to sell project management to senior executives."

Overall, the confidence in the robustness of the data output used to build the GENERAL SELLING BASE MODEL is high. Items that are not highlighted in the tables could be held to a rigorous 0.7 loading cut off. We used an acceptable cut off of 0.60 for our factor loadings, as discussed in Chapter 3. The items in Table 6.2 that are significant at a cut off of 0.60 loading are highlighted in light gray. These factors have the lowest significance in our analysis. Any factors with these loadings that only had one item greater than 0.6 are excluded, in keeping with factor analysis guidelines for rigor. The Kaiser-Meyer-Olkin Measure of Sampling Adequacy (KMO) was 0.937, indicating that the items that make up the factors explain a large part of the variance in understanding how to sell, as well as showing high reliability.

The following nine factors (factors 1–7 and 9–10, with 8 not being significant) were extracted from the rotated component matrix for the combined project personnel and consultant groups, with a sample size of 743 (one-half of the sample).

In interpreting each model, the first factor represents the items that, in general, explain most of the variance in the data. In the GENERAL SELLING BASE MODEL, the **Executive Framing** factor represents the *most common arguments and processes involved in selling project management today*. A couple of important insights come from looking at the **Executive Framing** factor. First, framing investment in project management as a senior executive decision, providing supporting evidence and facts, and using informal communication practices all appear important in the selling process. Second, in looking at the individual items (questions) grouped in this factor, the items clearly relate to packaging and explaining process concepts. Packaging arguments include those arguments describing project management in executive language and using words that the senior executives relate to and can easily understand. This set of arguments also included selling project management as *benefits* (e.g., long-term benefits, solution, and high payoff). Process concepts include describing how project management *fits with the corporate business goals*, and framing project management as a *solution*. The important mention of the use of *informal channels* hints at the underlying political channels that are exercised in successful sales efforts.

In the GENERAL SELLING BASE MODEL, the **Alignment** factor represents the second most common set of arguments and processes involved in selling project management today. Alignment, both of project management with corporate goals, and between executive expectations and realistic outcomes, is an important family of arguments in selling project management to senior executives. Talk about alignment (aligning project management with the firm's operational and strategic goals; aligning portfolios of projects and project management delivers success; and aligning executive expectations) explains a significant percentage of the variance in success in selling project management.

The **Value Statements** factor represents the third most common factor representing important arguments and processes involved in selling project management today. These include *outcomes of the efficiency and effectiveness nature*, and *results that can be measured* (either quantitatively or qualitatively). Examples include arguments about how to improve financial measures, staff growth and development, customer satisfaction, profits, market share, and the use of non-financial measures. The **Value Statements** factor can be considered both a set of cognitive arguments that increase success in selling project management, as well as a packaging approach whereby the project management issue is bundled with, or tied to, other issues (notably business results) important to the organization. The issue of branding may become quite important in arguments of this nature, to enable the seller to build an identity around and for the value of the project management "package."

The **Iron Triangle** factor represents the fourth most common grouping of factors that are involved in selling project management today. This fourth factor deals with project management practices and outcome measures, often colloquially

Figure 6.1. General Selling Base Model (743)

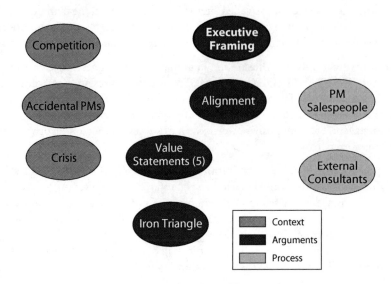

called the "iron triangle" of scope/quality, cost, and time constraints by practitioners. This factor points to those arguments including the expected outcomes of implementing project management, in terms of use of *appropriate tools and techniques and better schedule, budget, and scope outcomes*, as important in selling project management to senior executives.

The **Project Management Salespeople** factor represents the fifth most common process factor that is involved in selling project management today. The fifth factor suggests that *involving project personnel in the sales process* is an important part of selling project management to senior executives.

The **Competition** factor represents the sixth most common factor that is involved in selling project management today. This sixth factor deals with a contextual issue, identifying *competition* as a trigger for successfully interesting senior executives in project management.

The **Accidental Project Manager** factor represents the seventh most common factor that is involved in selling project management today. The seventh factor identifies the level of accidental project management practiced in the firm as an important contextual variable. This factor points to the presence of a context for selling where the seller has to be sensitive to, and aware that, the project managers may have little or no formal training, and that they might not be receiving due pay incentives. Thus, the salespeople must be aware and tailor the arguments appropriately. In light of the discussion on maturity models in Chapter 3, organizations sporting accidental project managers may be new to, or "green" at, managing projects or engrained in doing it one right way, not the most appropriate way.

The **External Consultants** factor represents the ninth most common process factor involved in selling project management today. The ninth factor indicates that the need to build a selling context that involves external consultants and marketers is also an important selling process. Combining the **External Consultants** factor with the **Project Management Personnel** factor points to the need to create a sales process that is relatively *inclusive, involving both internal and external resources*.

In the GENERAL SELLING BASE MODEL, the **Crisis** factor represents the tenth most common contextual factor involved in selling project management today. This factor suggests that organizational crisis is an important trigger for interest in project management.

Summary of GENERAL SELLING BASE MODEL

Another way to look at these factors is to distinguish amongst them by looking at those that relate to the selling context, those that describe the selling arguments, and those that examine the process. Figure 6.1 graphically depicts this analysis for GENERAL SELLING BASE MODEL.

Figure 6.1 depicts the most common contexts, arguments, and processes involved in selling project management, as reported by one-half of the project personnel and consulting respondents.

Project management is typically sold in a *context* where the role of project management as a competitive practice is important, where there is high recognition of accidental project managers, and there is strong perception of some sort of organizational crisis at play.

The most significant selling *arguments* involve framing project management as a senior executive decision using positive, executive language and linking it to long-term business objectives. The second most important set of arguments are those that align project management with other issues and outcomes important to the organization, including senior executive expectations with respect to project management. The ovals in Figure 6.1, labeled "executive framing" and "alignment," are placed closer to the process ovals (project management salespeople and external consultants) because these arguments could also be seen as selling strategies whereby sellers can align project management with corporate goals. Next, a large number of value statements (five as indicated in parenthesis in the figure) are used in, or as, selling arguments justifying the need for project management. These selling arguments include a wide range of options that any seller could arguably try, and link, to project management. These value statements may be heavily linked to the context and the ability of the salespersons themselves. Finally, the iron triangle outcomes and project management practices are presented as important sales arguments.

The most important processes, as shown in Figure 6.1, are those related to decisions about whom to involve in the sales process. Overall, inclusion seems to be the norm. Both internal and external project management personnel are considered important to the sales process.

The next section presents a discussion of the next model, the PROJECT PERSONNEL SELLING MODEL, followed by a discussion of the CONSULTANT SELLING MODEL. By comparing the output from these models, we reveal any differences in how project management is sold by these two groups.

PROJECT PERSONNEL SELLING MODEL (n = 499)

In the PROJECT PERSONNEL SELLING MODEL, seven factors were identified in helping to explain how project personnel sell project management. However, only six are statistically significant (the sixth factor was not significant). As described in the previous section, each factor received a descriptive label. Table 6.3 shows the six factors, corresponding item numbers, and items. Again, these factors, identified in the far left column of Table 6.3, are shown in order of importance, including: Executive Framing (most important), Alignment, Value Statements, Project Management Salespeople, Resistance to Project Management, and External Consultants (least important). As a whole, the six factors account for 52.0 percent of the variance, and the top three factors account for 40.1 percent of the variance. The KMO for this model is 0.935, indicating very strong reliability for the associations.

Not surprisingly, the results of this factor analysis are quite similar to the GENERAL SELLING BASE MODEL, given that project personnel make up the largest proportion of the sample. In fact, the first three factors (Executive Framing, Alignment, and Value Statements) are identical to and reflect the same ordering of importance as in the GENERAL SELLING BASE MODEL. It is in the differences that the interesting story is to be told. These differences are in both the relative explanatory power of the individual factors in the different models, and the importance of different items in the loadings (importance) on each factor. For example, the loadings of the specific items that account for the most variance in the top three factors in each model are different. For example in Table 6.2, the **Alignment** factor is most adeptly explained by item number 2_5, "Senior management's expectations are realistic," but in Table 6.3, item 3_1, "Project management is aligned with company's operational/business goals," has the greatest explanatory power (accounts for the highest percentage of the variance in the **Alignment** factor). The following interpretation focuses on these differences.

The composition of the **Executive Framing** factor in the PROJECT PERSONNEL SELLING MODEL is very similar to that of the GENERAL SELLING BASE MODEL, reinforcing the importance of using *executive language* in the sale of project management to make strong *benefit statements that fit with corporate business goals*. However, project personnel also refer to the importance of *using facts and evidence* to justify the benefits of project management. However, project personnel *do not* report framing project management as an executive decision, using informal communication channels, or describing

Table 6.3. Exploratory Factor Analysis for the Project Personnel Selling Model

Factor	Items	Items from Survey
1 Executive Framing	9_1	Successful approach—discuss how project management fits company's business
	9_6	Successful approach—executive is supportive, approachable
	10_4	Frame project management as uncovering issues, identifying solutions
	10_5	Frame project management as technique to achieve company mission or goals
	11_1	Describe project management with simple, clear language
	11_3	Describe project management with positive words (success, savings)
	11_4	Describe project management as contributing to firm's long-term benefits
	11_5	Describe project management using executive language
	11_7	Describe project management using supporting evidence, facts to justify value
	12_3	Link project management to corporate goals, business objectives
	10_1	Frame project management as having a high payoff with few negative consequences
	10_3	Present project management as a solution to a specific problem
2 Alignment	3_1	Project management is aligned with company's operational/business goals
	3_2	Project management is aligned with company's strategic goals
	3_6	Decision-makers consider cross project interactions
	4_5	Projects are aligned with company's strategic plans
	2_5	Senior management's expectations are realistic
	2_7	Senior management understands that project management is investment in long-term firm success
	3_5	Project management increases likelihood of delivering successful projects
3 Value Statements	6_1	Project management contributes to improved financial measures
	6_2	Project management enhances staff growth and development
	6_3	Project management enhances customer satisfaction, profits, market share
	6_5	Project management helps firm compete better than competition
	6_6	Project management enhances firm's non-financial performance
4 PM Framing	7_2	Effective selling of project management involves PMO staff
	7_3	Effective selling of project management involves project management staff
5 Resistance to Project Management	2_2	Selling project management is hard to do at our firm
	3_3	There is resistance to project management at our firm
6		NOT SIGNIFICANT
7 External Consultants	7_4	Effective selling involves external marketing/sales staff
	7_5	Effective selling involves external consultants

project management as a solution to a specific "point of pain" to sell project management to senior executives. Project personnel do make specific reference to *having a supportive context for the sales effort*, as indicated by the statement that the *senior executive is supportive and approachable* being a significant item in the **Executive Framing** factor in the PROJECT PERSONNEL SELLING MODEL. Thus, project personnel seem to be more attuned to contextual issues in the sales process, and seem less likely to use informal channels. They are also more likely to sell project management in relation to a specific organizational problem.

The second most important factor in the PROJECT PERSONNEL SELLING MODEL is the **Alignment** factor. Like the GENERAL SELLING BASE MODEL, the PROJECT PERSONNEL SELLING MODEL shows the importance of needing *alignment* between project management and corporate goals and executive expectations. The major difference between the **Alignment** factor in these two models is that, for the PROJECT PERSONNEL SELLING MODEL, statements about realistic senior executive expectations or funding of project management are not positively correlated with sales of project management to senior executives. Conversely, statements suggesting that *project management increases the likelihood of delivering successful projects* are correlated with the sale of project management in the PROJECT PERSONNEL SELLING MODEL.

The **Value Statement** factor is the third most important factor in both of these models, and it points to the identification of arguments about *outcomes of efficiency and effectiveness* and *results that can be measured* (either quantitatively or qualitatively) by using project management. As well, both models are identical in the use of cognitive arguments that increase success in selling project management, as well as a packaging approach whereby the project management issue is bundled with, or tied to, other issues (notably business results) important to the organization.

The **PM Framing** factor in the PROJECT PERSONNEL SELLING MODEL is the fourth most important factor, and it is the fifth most important factor in the GENERAL SELLING BASE MODEL. However, both point to the importance of *involving the project management office (PMO) and the project management staff* in the sales process context. Furthermore, both models contain the **External Consultant** factor. Considering the position of this factor near the end of the GENERAL SELLING BASE MODEL and at the end of the PROJECT PERSONNEL SELLING MODEL, this practice is important, but not as important as the other factors such as executive language, value statements, and so on. However, being *inclusive rather than exclusive* in the sales process is a significant practice. Overall, the similarities in the models show that both consultants and project personnel approach the sales process in similar ways with respect to who is included.

The **Resistance to Project Management** factor is fifth, and the only unique factor in the PROJECT PERSONNEL SELLING MODEL. Resistance deals with a contextual issue perceived by sellers to exist in the organization. Both items that make up this factor actually have negative scores implying that reported *resistance to project management reflects increased difficulty* in selling project management to senior executives. This result may seem obvious but, at the same time, in overlooking this factor, sellers may find the door shut if they do not slowly "warm up" the audience over time, rather than go for the one big sale.

Notably absent from this model are factors identified in the GENERAL SELLING BASE MODEL, including **Iron Triangle**, **Competition**, **Accidental Project Manager**, and **Crisis**. Overall, this seems to indicate that internal project management personnel do not focus on iron triangle descriptors of the outcomes of project management as a sales argument, and likewise may not focus on the triggers of increased competition, accidental project management, and organizational crisis.

There are many possible explanations for the absence of those factors in project personnel's sales approaches. Based on the findings from Phase I, the main reason may be that at the very time when crisis or accidental project management levels trigger senior executive interest in project management, internal project personnel credibility is at its lowest. Therefore, their sales efforts have other triggers. Reasons for project personnel not using iron triangle and competition arguments may relate to the absence or lack of business training to identify senior executive language to describe the use and purpose of iron triangle techniques, or to elucidate how project management could address competitive challenges. It may also suggest that the senior management plans and directions, related to corporate strategy, are not shared with those at the project management levels, proximally occupied by project personnel.

CONSULTANT SELLING MODEL (n = 244)

In the CONSULTANT SELLING MODEL, ten factors were identified in helping to explain how to sell. All ten factors are statistically significant. As described in the previous section, each factor received a descriptive label. Table 6.4 shows the ten factors, corresponding item numbers, and items. Again, these factors, identified in the far left column of Table 6.4, are shown in order of importance, including: Executive Framing (most important), Relationship, Value Statements, Iron Triangle, Alignment, Project Management Salespeople, Accidental Project Management, Competition, Executive Expectations, and Resistance to Project Management (least important). The ten factors account for 58.5 percent of the variance, and the top three factors account for 27.8 percent of the variance. The KMO was 0.880, reflecting strong reliability of the variance analysis model.

The CONSULTANT SELLING MODEL is similar to the GENERAL SELLING BASE MODEL and the PROJECT PERSONNEL SELLING MODEL, but again it is in the differences where the interest lies.

The most important factor is the **Executive Framing** factor, a finding that is identical to project personnel. Consultants primarily focus on describing how project management *fits with the corporate business* and identifying project management as offering *benefits* (i.e., long-term benefits, solution, and high payoff). The obvious difference is that the CONSULTANT SELLING MODEL does not contain reference to the importance of *using facts and evidence* to sell project management. More strongly, the CONSULTANT SELLING MODEL points to the use of *simple, clear language* or *using informal communication channels*. Unique to this model is the inclusion of items explicitly identifying the *use of a bundling strategy* that sellers use to tie project management to other strategies. A bundling approach may reflect the nature of consulting, and that project management is often sold as a component of a larger package, rather than as an initiative in its own right.

For the consultants, the **Relationship** factor explains the second largest part of the variance around selling. It refers to the *nature of the selling relationship*, including such items as *existing relationship, trustworthiness, supportiveness of the executive, and credibility*. It may be that the selling approaches used by consultants recognize the need to develop desirable relationship characteristics, something not found in the PROJECT PERSONNEL SELLING MODEL.

The **Value Statements** factor is the third most important in the CONSULTANT SELLING MODEL. Many of the arguments and processes used to describe project management are identical in content and placement to the GENERAL SELLING BASE MODEL and the PROJECT PERSONNEL SELLING MODEL. This finding underscores the importance of understanding value whether the seller is project personnel, consultant, or part of the internal project personnel.

The fourth factor relates to the **Iron Triangle**. Consultants appear to develop arguments around the iron triangle that are related to project management. This factor points to the use of *marketing promises of improved accountability, consistency, and predictability of results*. A key insight is that the **Iron Triangle** factor arguments are not part of the PROJECT PERSONNEL SELLING MODEL. It could be that promises of accountability are seen by senior executives as more credible coming from an external source. As well, the consequences of not delivering on iron triangle related promises might be too high of a risk for internal staff.

Alignment is the fifth most important factor for consultant selling arguments. However, in the CONSULTANT SELLING MODEL, the original **Alignment** factor is actually broken into two subsets by the factor analysis. Thus, the first subset of **Alignment** contains the consultant's selling arguments referring to *goal alignment*. The second subset of **Alignment** splits off into a separate factor, including other items, to create factor nine, the **Executive Expectations** factor. Clearly, consultant's arguments recognize the importance of senior management expectations, however, considering the difficulties experienced by consultants in selling project management, there may be quite a large knowing-doing gap—consultants may not actually manage senior executive expectations very well, particularly using goal alignment strategies that have been identified as important.

Consultants also recognize the importance of *using internal project management salespeople* in successfully selling project management, as reflected in the presence of the sixth factor, the **Project Management Salespeople** factor. This factor speaks to the importance of selling as an inclusive activity that involves different levels of contacts within the organization.

The **Competition** factor was identified as the eighth most important factor in the CONSULTANT SELLING MODEL. The factor indicates that consultants believe they can interest senior executives by speaking about past project successes, new business opportunity areas, and the competition. Again there may be a knowing-doing gap, since consultants tend to sell by using arguments about the competition on a tactical level even if they know from experience or know of cases where more strategic selling builds stronger long-term selling relationships. It may be that the costs of long-term relationship building makes selling on a tactical level seem like a more prudent sales investment. In a world where the low bidder wins

Table 6.4. Exploratory Factor Analysis for the Consultant Selling Model

Factor	Items	Items from Survey
1 Executive Framing	10_4	Frame project management as uncovering issues, identifying solutions
	10_1	Frame project management as having a high payoff with few negative consequences
	10_2	Frame project management as an executive decision
	10_3	Present project management as a solution to a specific problem
	10_5	Frame project management as technique to achieve company mission or goals
	11_3	Describe project management with positive words (success, savings)
	11_4	Describe project management contributing to firm's long-term benefits
	12_2	Bundle project management with other strategies being brought to executive attention
	12_3	Link project management to corporate goals, business objectives
	12_4	Describe project management's value as fixing a specific "point of pain"
2 Relationship	9_1	Successful approach—discuss how project management fits company's business
	9_3	Successful approach—had existing business relationship
	9_4	Successful approach—seller is credible
	9_5	Successful approach—seller is trustworthy
	9_6	Successful approach—executive is supportive, approachable
3 Value Statements	6_1	Project management enhances staff growth and development
	6_2	Project management contributes to improved financial measures
	6_3	Project management enhances customer satisfaction, profits, market share
	6_5	Project management helps firm compete better than competition
	6_6	Project management enhances firm's non-financial performance
4 Iron Triangle	4_2	Projects at firm are completed on schedule
	4_3	Projects at firm are completed on budget
	4_4	Projects at firm are completed within objectives (scope)
	4_1	Projects are managed with appropriate tools, techniques, and methodologies
5 Alignment	3_1	Project management is aligned with company's operational/business goals
	3_2	Project management is aligned with company's strategic goals
6 Project Management Salespeople	7_1	Effective selling of project management involves middle managers
	7_2	Effective selling of project management involves PMO staff
	7_3	Effective selling of project management involves project management staff
7 Accidental Project Manager	5_1	PMs have little or no formal training in the discipline
	5_2	People are assigned project management titles without promotions or pay increases
8 Competition	8_1	Executive interested in project management when the competition is doing better
	8_2	Senior executives interested in project management when they see new business opportunities
	8_4	Senior executives interested in project management when they hear about internal project successes
9 Senior Executive Expectations	2_5	Senior management expectations are realistic
	2_6	Senior management expectations are attainable
10 Resistance to Project Management	2_2	Selling project management is hard to do at our firm
	3_3	There is resistance to project management at our firm

the work most often, long-term, strategic relationship building may fall prey to tight bottom line requirements.

The CONSULTANT SELLING MODEL also identified the **Accidental Project Manager** factor as important to the sales process. As discussed, the term accidental project manager refers to project managers that have little or no formal training, and have been given titles without promotions or pay increases to manage strategically important projects. The presence of this factor may speak to the need for consultants to be aware of, and ready to shift, selling approaches to the level of the internal project manager, who may not have formal training and/or education in project management. At the same time, this finding may indicate that consultants view the accidental project manager context as being a favorable one in which to sell project management to senior executives.

Notably absent from this model is a factor relating to crisis as a trigger for increased senior executive interest in project management.

Summary of GENERAL SELLING BASE MODEL, PROJECT PERSONNEL SELLING MODEL, and CONSULTANT SELLING MODEL

In summary, this section presented the findings and interpretations of data that identified the most common arguments, processes, and contexts of how to sell project management to senior executives. The analysis and interpretation provide a "snapshot" in time of the general environment in which project management is sold in organizations, and the most common arguments and processes used today.

Overall, the GENERAL SELLING BASE MODEL, the CONSULTANT SELLING MODEL, and the PROJECT PERSONNEL SELLING MODEL, indicate that project personnel and consultants stress different arguments, as well as different aspects of similar arguments, in selling project management. One of the most significant differences to come to light is the project personnel's emphasis on alignment and value statements, and the consultants' focus on the relationship aspects of selling. Conceivably, project personnel could improve their sales attempts by paying more attention to using successful arguments to build selling relationships; and consultants could improve their efforts by working on aligning project management with the specific corporate goals of the target organization. One barrier to relationship building for project personnel lies in establishing credibility to gain access to senior executives. As established in the Phase I research, internal project personnel may be one of the primary sources of immediate information in a crisis situation, and thus, the risk of something going wrong and being tied to the internal project manager may, in effect, hinder later relationship-building efforts.

The next section presents the findings that point to the "best practices" or most successful arguments, processes, and contexts in selling project management to senior executives.

How Do We *Successfully* Sell Project Management to Senior Executives?

The initial analysis of these models contains the most commonly reported factors representing the arguments and processes most commonly employed, in the key contexts of interest. The next task is to examine and discuss the data obtained from those who reported being very successful in selling project management to senior executives or very unsuccessful.

Each of the next sections begins with a brief introduction to the participant demographics, and concludes with the presentation, analysis, and discussion of the findings within the EFA models. We look at the VERY SUCCESSFUL SELLING BASE MODEL, the VERY SUCCESSFUL PROJECT PERSONNEL MODEL, the VERY SUCCESSFUL CONSULTANT MODEL, and finally the VERY UNSUCCESSFUL SELLING MODEL. The output of this analysis helps us identify the most common "best practices" used by very successful sellers, whether consultants or project personnel.

VERY SUCCESSFUL SELLING BASE MODEL (n = 99)

As a first cut, we looked at who is very successful at selling project management to senior executives. Overall, slightly more than three-quarters (76 percent) of project personnel and consultants believe that they have been somewhat successful in selling project management to senior executives, but only 13 percent report being very successful. The demographics of those reporting being very successful are reported in the following section.

Demographics

- Fifty-eight are over forty (58.6 percent).

- Seventy-five are male (75.8 percent) and twenty-three female (23.2 percent).

- Fifty-eight (58.6 percent) are from Canada and thirty-two (32.3 percent) are from the United States.

- Four (4 percent) have less than five years of experience, and twenty (20.2 percent) had over sixteen years of experience with their current employer.

- Fifty-three have only individual courses in project management education (53.5 percent).

- Sixty-three (63.6 percent) belong to a project management association.

- Nineteen (19.2 percent) hold professional certification.

- Sixty-eight (68.7 percent) spend over 50 percent of their time on project management and fifty-seven (57.6 percent) expect to spend more time on project management in the future (somewhat likely and very likely).

In general, the demographics for very successful sellers are similar to the population demographics, with a couple of notable exceptions. First, the very successful selling group has a slightly higher propensity to belong to a project management association, be male, and have more (5–10 years) experience with their current employer. At the same time, their level of project management certification, proportion with single courses or no formal project management training, and years of work experience are almost the same as the sample population. In short, the very successful sellers are quite experienced, gaining much of this knowledge from individual courses and practical work experience. Second, this male dominant group (75 percent) has slightly more project management experience than the general sample population, and is slightly more likely to come from Canada.

VERY SUCCESSFUL SELLING BASE MODEL Findings

The VERY SUCCESSFUL SELLING BASE MODEL is derived from data supplied by all project personnel and consultants who reported being very successful in selling project management to senior executives. Eight factors were identified as helping to explain how to successfully sell project management. All eight factors are statistically significant. As described in the previous sections, each factor received a descriptive label. Table 6.5 shows the eight factors, corresponding item numbers, and items. Again, these factors, identified in the far left column of Table 6.5, are shown in order of importance, including: Value Statements (most important), Iron Triangle, Executive Language, Relationship, Senior Management Expectations, Corporate Fit, Executive Decision, and Resistance to Project Management (least important). The eight factors, as a whole, account for 59.8 percent of the variance, and the top three factors account for 30.5 percent of the variance. The KMO was 0.782, reflecting a very reliable and statistically robust factor model.

The first factor in the VERY SUCCESSFUL SELLING BASE MODEL is the **Value Statements** factor. This finding is not surprising, considering that the most common arguments for all groups of sellers also note the importance of value statements. However, the very successful sellers, as shown in Table 6.5, relate value statements to *business results*. Those very successful in selling use arguments that speak to *outcomes of the efficiency and effectiveness type*, and *to results that can be measured* either quantitatively or qualitatively. Examples include improved financial measures, staff growth and development, customer satisfaction, profits, market share, and non-financial measures. From this data, we infer that using value statements, like these examples identified in the selling process, is positively related to success in selling project management to senior executives.

The second most important factor reflects a focus on project outcomes, as shown by the presence of the **Iron Triangle** factor. Very successful selling arguments are crafted around how project management can bring projects in *on time, on budget, and within scope and quality specifications*. Again, this factor reflects important and successful selling arguments related to *the bottom line, project success, and meeting expectations*.

The third factor deals with processes of selling. The presence of the **Executive Language** factor points to the ability to *sell the benefits*, not simply the features, of project management. Very successful sellers *use words that the senior executives relate to*, and they describe and sell project management as *offering benefits* (e.g., long-term benefits, solution, high payoff). As

Table 6.5. Exploratory Factor Analysis for Very Successful Selling Base Model

Factor	Items	Items on Survey
1 Value Statements	6_1	Project management contributes to improved financial measures
	6_2	Project management enhances staff growth and development
	6_3	Project management enhances customer satisfaction, profits, market share
	6_5	Project management helps firm compete better than competition
	6_6	Project management enhances firm's non-financial performance
2 Iron Triangle	4_1	Projects are managed with appropriate tools, techniques, and methodologies
	4_2	Projects at firm are completed on schedule
	4_3	Projects at firm are completed on budget
	4_4	Projects at firm are completed within objectives (scope)
3 Executive Language	11_1	Describe project management with simple, clear language
	11_3	Describe project management with positive words (success, savings)
	11_4	Describe project management as contributing to firm's long-term benefits
	11_5	Describe project management using executive language
	11_7	Describe project management using supporting evidence, facts to justify value
4 Relationship	9_3	Successful approach—had existing business relationship
	9_4	Successful approach—seller is credible
	9_5	Successful approach—seller is trustworthy
	9_6	Successful approach—executive is supportive, approachable
5 Senior Management Expectations	2_4	Senior management approves adequate funding for project management
	2_5	Senior management's expectations are realistic
	2_6	Senior management's expectations are attainable
	2_7	Senior management understands that project management is investment in long-term firm success
6 Corporate Fit	10_5	Frame project management as technique to achieve company mission or goals
	12_1	Use informal communication practices, e.g., discuss in hallways
	12_3	Link project management to corporate goals, business objectives
7 Executive Decision	10_2	Frame project management as a senior executive decision
	10_3	Present project management as a solution to a specific problem
8 Resistance to Project Management	2_2	Selling project management is hard to do at our firm
	3_3	There is resistance to project management at our firm

shown in the initial GENERAL SELLING BASE MODEL, executive language is only a subset of the **Executive Framing** factor. The key point is that using appropriate executive language accounts for a significant percentage of the variance, or ability to explain very successful selling arguments, in the sale of project management.

The fourth factor (**Relationship**) that the very successful project personnel and consultants focus on is building *effective relationships* with the buyer *involving credibility and trustworthiness*, usually made easier by a previously established relationship. Considering the experience level of very successful sellers, buyer relationships may be less likely to be new "cold calls," and if they are, buyers may use branding, whereby they identify the seller as a trusted and credible source, based on reputation, thus, enabling the sale.

Figure 6.2. Very Successful Selling Base Model (99)

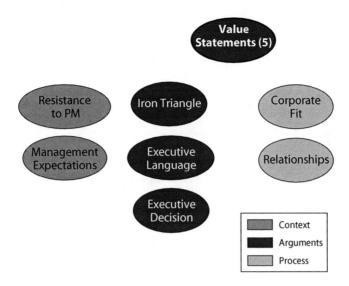

The next three factors reflect the importance of relating project management to the executive interests and expectations. The model indicates that very successful sellers focus on arguments and processes within each of these factors (**Executive Expectation**, **Corporate Fit**, and **Executive Decision**). Arguments and processes that manage executive expectations around project management, tie those expectations to corporate goals and objectives, and frame the decision to invest in project management as an executive decision, all speak to executives at the right level to lead to action. The **Executive Decision** is also a subset of the **Executive Framing** identified in the GENERAL SELLING BASE MODEL. This finding points to the importance of framing project management in ways that senior executives are interested in and can relate to in the most common selling arguments. However, the key part of the very successful selling argument, with respect to executive decisions, lies in framing selling arguments as senior executive decisions (strategic level), as well as solutions to specific problems (tactical/operational level), reflecting an interesting juxtaposition of interests.

Factor eight, **Resistance to Project Management**, speaks to the important recognition made by very successful sellers, that the selling context must be taken into consideration. Both items in this factor are negative scores, indicating that resistance to project management reflects increased difficulty in selling project management to senior executives. Although this factor seems to be on the minds of very successful sellers, it is the least critical of the factors in the model.

Figure 6.2 presents a graphical view of the discussion of very successful selling, of the salient context within which project management is sold, as well as the arguments and processes. The sample size for this analysis is ninety-nine, as indicated in the figure.

Those people reporting being very successful in selling project management to senior executives recognize the context as setting and managing realistic senior management expectations of project management, and creating or entering an environment that has little resistance to project management. These sellers tend to use arguments that highlight a variety of value statements (five as indicated in Figure 6.2) about financial measures, staff growth, customer satisfaction, competition, and non-financial performance, and then link them to issues/values of interest to the organization, thus, making the value statements also play a bundling role in the sales process. They also use project management outcomes and practices as important sales arguments. Although very successful sellers' arguments are sensitive to project management as a senior executive decision, they frame it in positive business language that speaks to solving problems. In terms of process, very successful sellers focus on explaining the fit between project management and the corporation or organization. Ultimately, very successful sellers pay attention to the quality of the relationship and, in building that relationship, may be more adept at shifting arguments as the business context changes over time, thus, creating lasting buyer-seller relations.

In comparing The VERY SUCCESSFUL SELLING BASE MODEL with the GENERAL SELLING BASE MODEL, the main arguments for selling project management to senior executives are very similar in both models. However, the very successful sellers report using much more consistent and refined arguments, that include value statements, iron triangle, executive language, executive expectations, corporate fit, and project management as an executive decision. Although common selling arguments include all these aspects, the major difference is that very successful sellers tend to individually recognize each type of argument. This distinction indicates that very successful sellers know exactly what emphasis to put on the selling argument, and do so in making the sale. Essentially, the results indicate that very successful sellers know what to do and do it—thus, effectively bridging a knowing-doing gap. In addition, the very successful model points to the importance of the selling relationship in the sales process that is not present in the GENERAL SELLING BASE MODEL or the PROJECT PERSONNEL SELLING MODEL.

Finally, the **Accidental Project Manager** factor, reference to involving external and internal personnel, and selling on the basis of *crisis-driven* sales to trigger senior executive interest are not part of the VERY SUCCESSFUL SELLING BASE MODEL. There are a number of interpretations that could be made. One suggests that very successful sellers are in, or sell to, mature project management firms. These firms have invested, or are investing, in their staff's project management training and education, and are not rife with crises or vulnerable to being easily triggered into a crisis by an internal or external event. This assertion bears further examination of the data for support.

Next, we separated the very successful *project personnel* from the very successful *consultants* to identify differences between these groups as compared to the "best" practices identified by the VERY SUCCESSFUL SELLING BASE MODEL. The next section begins with a brief introduction to the participant demographics, and concludes with the presentation, analysis, and discussion of the findings within the very successful selling models.

VERY SUCCESSFUL PROJECT PERSONNEL MODEL (N = 61)

What are the characteristics of sixty-one very successful project personnel? The following section provides a brief review of the demographics of this group, as compared to other groups in this study. The most interesting areas of comparison are discussed.

Demographics
Demographics of those in the VERY SUCCESSFUL PROJECT PERSONNEL MODEL are as follows:

- Thirty are over forty years of age (49.2 percent). This group is slightly younger than the general respondents, where 63 percent are over forty.

- There are forty-four males (72.1 percent) and seventeen females (27.9 percent). This compares to the demographics of the general respondents.

- Thirty-six (59 percent) are from Canada and twenty-one (34.4 percent) are from the United States. This compares to the demographics of the very successful sellers.

- Three (4.9 percent) have less than five years of experience, whereas five (8.2 percent) have over sixteen years of experience.

- Thirty-seven (60.7 percent) have only individual course project management training. This figure is higher than that for the general project personnel demographic profile, which indicated that 56 percent had no more than individual courses.

- Thirty-four (55.7 percent) belong to a project management association. This figure is slightly higher than that for the project personnel group as a whole (51 percent).

- Sixteen (9.8 percent) have professional certification. This figure is lower than that for the project personnel demographics, indicating that 17 percent have project management designations.

- Forty-four (72.1 percent) spend over 50 percent of their time on project management and thirty-seven (60.7 percent) expect to spend more time on project management in the future (somewhat likely and very likely).

In general, this group is slightly younger than the total sample population, slightly more likely to spend the majority of their time on project management, and less likely to hold a professional project management designation. They have between six and fifteen years project management experience, and tend to have only single course preparation in project management. This indicates that a high proportion of project personnel who report being very successful in selling project management to senior executives would fit into the accidental project manager category.

The next section presents the specific arguments, context, and processes that the results show as significant in the VERY SUCCESSFUL PROJECT PERSONNEL MODEL.

VERY SUCCESSFUL PROJECT PERSONNEL MODEL Findings

In the VERY SUCCESSFUL PROJECT PERSONNEL MODEL, five factors were identified as helping to explain how to successfully sell project management. All five factors are statistically significant. As described in the previous sections, each factor received a descriptive label. Table 6.6 shows the five factors, corresponding item numbers, and items. Again, these factors, identified in the far left column of Table 6.6, are shown in order of importance, including: Iron Triangle (most important), Relationship, Executive Framing, Value Statements, and Senior Management Expectations (least important). These five factors account for 66 percent of the variance, and the top three factors account for 46.8 percent of the variance. The KMO was 0.773, showing high reliability of the factor model.

These findings highlight an interesting difference between project personnel's selling efforts, in general, as compared to very successful project personnel. The data reported in Table 6.6 shows that the **Iron Triangle** factor explains the most variance in the VERY SUCCESSFUL PROJECT PERSONNEL MODEL. Interestingly, the PROJECT PERSONNEL SELLING MODEL (Table 6.3) does not identify an **Iron Triangle** factor.

This is a surprise finding, as we initially thought that senior executives would not be interested in detailed discussions of project management practices. However, analysis of the qualitative responses of these project personnel potentially sheds some light on this finding. Compared to the conventional understanding of the iron triangle, very successful project personnel seem to use slightly modified iron triangle arguments that are more closely *tied to the strategic end of the business*. This learning may come from the intense and hands-on involvement of project personnel with the traditional methods and practices of project management. The key point is that this group may have learned to make connections, or know how to teach senior executives to make connections, between the use of tools and techniques and the strategic value of project management.

Overall, the data in this factor indicates that this group knows how to sell tactically, and they do it well. By tactical selling, we refer to focusing on arguments concerning the operational aspects of project management. However, the findings also show that this group does not stick to one selling approach, thus, within the tactical arena, many different operational type arguments may be used in selling. Thus, this group does not use a single approach to sell.

The second factor identified by this analysis, in order of importance, is the **Relationship** factor. The results indicate that the very successful project personnel emphasize the relationship processes. This data identifies having an *effective, credible relationship* with the buyer as an important process in selling project management to senior executives. Conversely, the general PROJECT PERSONNEL SELLING MODEL, for the sample as a whole, does not contain a **Relationship** factor. This result shows the importance project personnel who are very successful in interesting senior executives in project management place on the softer, or social, aspects of selling that are fundamentally tied to success regardless of whether you work within or outside the organization.

Both the PROJECT PERSONNEL SELLING MODEL and the VERY SUCCESSFUL PROJECT PERSONNEL MODEL reflect the importance of the **Executive Framing** factor in selling project management to senior executives. However, executive framing in the very successful sellers' arguments is somewhat different. Successful project personnel frame project management in a slightly narrower context as an *executive decision* and as a *solution to a problem* in *simple, clear language*. They also *emphasize* that tools and techniques are important. These findings indicate that this group is readily able to adapt arguments to manage senior management expectations.

The **Value Statements** factor is present in the PROJECT PERSONNEL SELLING MODEL, as well as the VERY SUCCESSFUL PROJECT PERSONNEL MODEL. However, in the very successful model, sellers focus on a smaller set of value statement-type arguments than those identified by the PROJECT PERSONNEL SELLING MODEL. Very successful

Table 6.6. Exploratory Factor Analysis for the Very Successful Project Personnel Model

Factor	Items	Items from Survey
1 Iron Triangle	3_6	Decision-makers consider cross-project interactions
	4_1	Projects are managed with appropriate tools, techniques, and methodologies
	4_2	Projects at firm are completed on schedule
	4_3	Projects at firm are completed on budget
	4_4	Projects at firm are completed within objectives (scope)
	4_5	Projects are aligned with company's strategic plans
2 Relationship	9_1	Successful approach—discuss how project management fits company's business
	9_4	Successful approach—seller is credible
	9_5	Successful approach—seller is trustworthy
	9_6	Successful approach—executive is supportive, approachable
3 Executive Framing	10_2	Frame project management as an executive decision
	10_3	Present project management as a solution to a specific problem
	11_1	Describe project management with simple, clear language
	11_6	Describe project management by emphasizing detailed features, tools, techniques
4 Value Statements	6_2	Project management enhances staff growth and development
	6_3	Project management enhances customer satisfaction, profits, market share
	6_5	Project management helps firm compete better than competition
5 Senior Management Expectations	2_5	Senior management's expectations are realistic
	2_6	Senior management's expectations are attainable

project personnel stress project management value through *enhancing staff growth and development, customer satisfaction, profits, market share, and beating the competition*. Lastly, the very successful project personnel emphasize *realistic and attainable senior management expectations*.

Notably absent from this model is any recognition of **Resistance to Project Management**. This likely indicates that those project personnel who are very successful in selling project management to senior executives are operating in a more favorable project management context than is generally found across the organizations in our sample.

Figure 6.3 presents the key contexts, arguments, and processes for this group of sixty-one participants (sample noted in title).

In summary, the very successful project personnel emphasize the importance of realistic senior executive expectations in providing a supportive selling context. They report using iron triangle arguments that are tied to project outcomes and practices as the most important selling arguments. They tend to frame project management as an executive decision and as a way to solve a specific problem. They focus on three important value statements (noted in Figure 6.3 and discussed previously). Since this is often paradoxical, they seem to know when to use a specific tactical argument and they do it well. They also use simple, clear business language to explain the project management tools and techniques in some detail,

Figure 6.3. Very Successful Project Personnel Model (61)

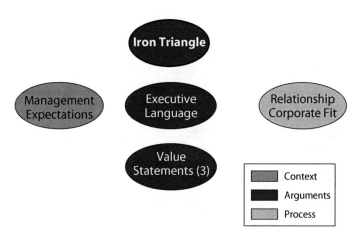

keeping the tie to business objectives in mind. They also focus on the relationship processes and, to a lesser degree, the fit of project management to the organization. Overall, selling in this group is a multifactorial process, based on context and content, and involving a strong relationship component.

VERY SUCCESSFUL CONSULTANT MODEL (n = 38)

This next section begins with a brief introduction to the participant demographics of the VERY SUCCESSFUL CONSULTANT MODEL, and concludes with the presentation, analysis, and discussion of the findings within the very successful selling model for this group.

Demographics
This group consisted of thirty-eight consultants. Key demographics for the consultants reporting very high success rates in selling project management to senior executives are as follows:

- Twenty-eight are over forty (73.7 percent).

- Thirty-one are male (81.6 percent) and six are female (15.8 percent).

- Twenty-two (57.9 percent) are from Canada and eleven (28.9 percent) are from the United States.

- Three (7.9 percent) have less than five years of experience, while twenty-four (63.2 percent) have over sixteen years of experience.

- Sixteen have only individual courses in project management education (42.1 percent).

- Twenty-nine consultants (76.3 percent) belong to a project management association.

- Thirteen (34.2 percent) hold professional certification.

This group is slightly older than the very successful project personnel group, where only 49 percent were over forty. Compared to the very successful project personnel, there are more consultants with over sixteen years of experience. The male-female ratio follows the same trends for the other groups. The proportion of consultants belonging to a professional association and holding professional certification is much higher than for the project personnel group. This group also has more training than the very successful project personnel group. In addition, the vast majority of these consultants came from smaller companies.

VERY SUCCESSFUL CONSULTANT MODEL Findings
In the VERY SUCCESSFUL CONSULTANT MODEL, seven factors were identified in helping to explain how to successfully sell project management. As described in the previous sections, each factor received a descriptive label. Table 6.7

Table 6.7. Exploratory Factor Analysis for the Very Successful Consultant Model

Factor	Items	Items from Survey
1 Value Statements	6_1	Project management contributes to improved financial measures
	6_2	Project management enhances staff growth and development
	6_3	Project management enhances customer satisfaction, profits, market share
	6_4	Project management is a valued discipline like finance, engineering, IT
	6_5	Project management helps firm compete better than competition
	6_6	Project management enhances firm's non-financial performance
2 Executive Language	7_2	Effective selling of project management involves PMO staff
	7_3	Effective selling of project management involves project management staff
	11_1	Describe project management with simple, clear language
	11_3	Describe project management with positive words (success, savings)
	11_4	Describe project management contributing to firm's long-term benefits
	11_5	Describe project management using executive language
3 Iron Triangle	4_1	Projects are managed with appropriate tools, techniques, and methodologies
	4_2	Projects at firm are completed on schedule
	4_3	Projects at firm are completed on budget
	4_4	Projects at firm are completed within objectives (scope)
4 Alignment	3_1	Project management is aligned with company's operational/business goals
	3_2	Project management is aligned with company's strategic goals
	4_5	Projects are aligned with company's strategic plans
5 Relationship	9_3	Successful approach—had existing business relationship
	9_4	Successful approach—seller is credible
	9_5	Successful approach—seller is trustworthy
	9_6	Successful approach—executive is supportive, approachable
6 Accidental Project Manager	5_1	Project managers have little or no formal training in the discipline
	5_2	People are assigned project management titles without promotions or pay increases
7 Motivation	2_1	Selling project management to senior executives is an important issue to my organization
	8_1	Executive interested in project management when the competition is doing better

shows the seven factors, corresponding item numbers, and items. Again, these factors, identified in the far left column of Table 6.7, are shown in order of importance, including Value Statements (most important), Executive Language, Iron Triangle, Alignment, Relationship, Accidental Project Management, and Motivation (least important). The seven factors account for 56.2 percent of the variance, and the top three factors account for 46.8 percent of the variance. Due to the small number of cases, there was no KMO score. This outcome means that the model is not as reliable as the others, and should be considered as a preliminary working model. It is included in this report for completeness and for discussion purposes.

The most important factor that very successful consultants have in common is the **Value Statement** factor. The model suggests that very successful consultants identify with all the potential value statements related to project management, resulting in a mixed bag of ways to convey the benefits and features of project management. Analysis of the qualitative data suggests that consultants who are very successful in selling project management are prepared to use any of these value statements with each potential client, but focus very quickly on the value statements most appropriate for the situation at hand.

The second factor, **Executive Language**, in the VERY SUCCESSFUL CONSULTANT MODEL is a combination of descriptive language that emphasizes *using simple, clear language, executive language, and positive words, describing long-term benefits, and involving the internal project management personnel.* This factor suggests that consultants see the use of executive language and the inclusiveness of the process as important and related factors in the selling process.

The third factor, **Iron Triangle**, reflects an emphasis on using iron triangle descriptors (i.e., that projects are completed on time, cost, and within scope and quality specifications). This information shows an interesting difference between the consultants and the project personnel both in the position of this factor in the model (in third place versus first place) and in the contents of the factor. The consultants' **Iron Triangle** factor is focused much more tightly on more traditional tactical or efficiency-based arguments.

Very successful consultants use the **Alignment** factor to sell project management, *emphasizing how project management is connected to the firm's operational and strategic goals.* Note that this factor is not evident in the VERY SUCCESSFUL PROJECT PERSONNEL MODEL. This difference may exist because consultants focus more time on selling how project management can align the tactical and strategic levels of the organization, instead of spending time on setting and managing senior executive expectations as a way of aligning, which is a key context factor in the VERY SUCCESSFUL PROJECT PERSONNEL MODEL.

Like the VERY SUCCESSFUL PROJECT PERSONNEL MODEL, the VERY SUCCESSFUL CONSULTANT MODEL shows the presence of a **Relationship** factor. This fifth factor for very successful consultants deals with developing relationships and having an effective, credible relationship with the buyer in the sales process.

The VERY SUCCESSFUL CONSULTANT MODEL also identifies the **Accidental Project Manager** factor and a **Motivation** factor. This result indicates that the consultants recognize the presence or absence of accidental project managers as a contextual variable to be considered in the sales process. It could be that the consultants need to frame arguments that are simple enough for a less educated or trained staff who do project management. They also note that selling project management is an important issue to their firm. Again, we cannot make statistical assumptions about this factor at this time. The dataset did not collect information on incentives to sell, but incentives could be a latent factor that consultants brought out as important. This outcome in itself is a very important finding that should be examined in subsequent research.

Figure 6.4 presents the graphic version of the context, arguments, and process data analyzed for very successful consultant selling.

Very successful consultants describe the selling context as including a high degree of accidental project managers and that project management is an important competitive issue. Although the model has weak statistical support at best, these findings are congruent with the selling decision-making process identified in Phase I, in relation to the type of consultants that are used to help organizations in crises to train staff or help grow project management internally.

They report using six value statements in making sales arguments that focus on using executive language and looking at long-term benefits. They seem adept at using arguments that convey the features of project management tools and/or use arguments that deal with outcomes of project management. In addition, alignment between management expectations and corporate goals are both reported as important and, again, interpreted as both arguments and strategic sales approaches. Finally, they recognize the importance of the relationship to the sales effort. In qualitative commentary provided in the survey, many of these participants made statements about the need to tailor their argument and process to the client they are working with. Statements such as "our clients cover the full spectrum, so the sell to them varies with their need and situation" are representative of this approach.

Thus, there do appear to be significant differences between the factors explaining the selling context, arguments, and processes between the CONSULTANT SELLING MODEL and the VERY SUCCESSFUL CONSULTANT MODEL, and between the VERY SUCCESSFUL PROJECT PERSONELL MODEL and the VERY SUCCESSFUL CONSULTANT MODEL. Overall, we conclude that best practices in selling project management do indeed exist, but these best practices are most tightly associated with the differences in the ways in which project personnel and consultants successfully sell project management.

Figure 6.4. Very Successful Consultant Model (38)

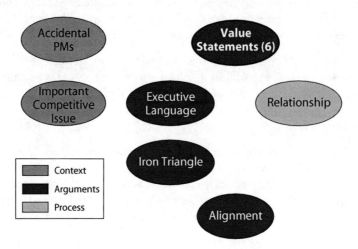

UNSUCCESSFUL SELLING MODEL (n = 19)

The next section presents the VERY UNSUCCESSFUL SELLING MODEL. This model is constructed to highlight whether there are any identifiable unsuccessful practices, by examining the context and practices of those declaring themselves extremely unsuccessful in selling project management to senior executives.

Due to the small sample size (n = 19), separate factor analysis could not be run on the very unsuccessful project personnel and the very unsuccessful consultants. Thus, there is no way to differentiate between these groups in the VERY UNSUCCESSFUL SELLING MODEL. First, let's explore the demographics for this group.

Demographics

This group consisted of nineteen (thirteen project personnel [68.4 percent] and six consultants [31.6 percent]).

- In total, thirteen are over forty years (68.4 percent).

- Fourteen are male (73.7 percent) and five are female (26.3 percent).

- Eight are from Canada (42.1 percent) and eleven are from the United States (57.9 percent).

- Nine have less than five years of experience (47.4 percent), and four have over sixteen years of experience (21 percent).

- Eleven (57.9 percent) have only individual courses in project management.

- Three have an undergraduate degree (15.8 percent).

- Nine (47.4 percent) belong to a project management association, and 10.5 percent have a professional certification.

- Nine (47.4 percent) spend over 50 percent of their time on project management, and thirteen expect to spend more time on project management in the future (68.4 percent).

The most noticeable difference, individually, is that this group is slightly older than the very successful sales people, noticeably less experienced in project management, and less likely to belong to a professional association or hold project manager certification. They are also somewhat less likely to spend the majority of their time on project management than the sample as a whole. Finally, they may come from different types and sizes of organizations than the rest of the sample. Only 30 percent of these individuals came from the six industries that covered one-half of our respondents. In addition, there was not as normal a spread in organizational size for this group. These individuals tended to come from very large or very small organizations. Again, this outcome could be a result of the small sample size or it could suggest that individuals in very small or very large organizations are less likely to be involved in project management, and have a harder time selling project management to their senior executives. This question needs to be examined with a larger sample size.

Keeping in mind that this group is a very small one from which to draw inferences, we note the importance in the process of analyzing this data in building theory.

VERY UNSUCCESSFUL SELLING MODEL Findings

In the VERY UNSUCCESSFUL SELLING MODEL, seven factors were identified in helping to explain how to successfully sell project management. Due to the small sample size, the KMO was not applicable, as it was positive definite. This situation means that these results are tenuous and the model is included as a working model only for discussion purposes.

As described in the previous sections, each factor received a descriptive label. Table 6.8 shows the seven factors, corresponding item numbers, and items. Again, these factors, identified in the far left column of Table 6.8, are shown in order of importance, including: Executive Framing (most important), PM Framing, Alignment, Iron Triangle, Resistance to Project Management, Senior Management Expectations, and Value Statements (least important). The top seven factors account for 84.9 percent of the variance, and the top three factors account for 44.5 percent of the variance.

The first factor for the VERY UNSUCCESSFUL SELLING MODEL combines a "hodgepodge" of points from the **Executive Framing** factor, but includes interesting and original points. It was not possible to identify a key theme from the points, and this outcome may be where their problem lies. The items covered in unsuccessful selling include *using executive language, presenting project management as a solution, speaking to the industry competition using dramatic terms, and talking about the value of project management, mainly in traditional iron triangle types of arguments.*

A key difference between the very unsuccessful group and the very successful project personnel/consultant groups is that the latter presented their points in ways that clustered meaningfully. Another important difference is that the emphasis in unsuccessful selling arguments is on *dramatic language and emotional terms*. This approach was not identified in any of the other analysis.

The second factor, labeled **PM Framing** in the model, includes both a statement on including project management personnel in the sales process, and two statements about the need to frame project management as a way to uncover issues and as a technique to achieve the company mission or goals. This situation may indicate that unsuccessful sellers turn to project management staff as a source of key information about the company's strategic goals in order to frame arguments about how project management will help senior executives identify problems and solutions.

Unsuccessful sellers also try to shape arguments around both operational and strategic alignment issues. This divides their focus, rendering them less effective in interesting senior executives, particularly because they tend to couch both types of arguments in iron triangle terms, focusing on tactical level improvements.

Unlike the very successful sellers (project personnel and consultant groups), resistance to project management is a contextual factor for unsuccessful sellers. The presence of the **Resistance to Project Management** factor in the VERY UNSUCCESSFUL SELLING MODEL indicates that those who were very unsuccessful in selling project management are operating in, or helping to create, a more difficult climate in which to promote project management.

The sixth factor is identified as the **Senior Management Expectations** factor. This contextual factor is not significant for the very successful consultants, and it is the last factor in the VERY SUCCESSFUL PROJECT PERSONNEL MODEL. This outcome may indicate again that the unsuccessful project personnel within the model are selling in a more difficult climate, possibly because they suffer from lower credibility when selling in times of organizational crises.

Finally, the **Value Statements** factor is the last factor in the VERY UNSUCCESSFUL SELLING MODEL. Conversely, this is the first factor in the VERY SUCCESSFUL CONSULTANT MODEL, and fourth on the list for the VERY SUCCESSFUL PROJECT PERSONNEL MODEL. The data shows that value statements are core to common selling arguments regardless of who is selling, and they are even more critical to very successful consultants. Although unsuccessful sellers report that they form arguments around effectiveness and innovation-type value related to customer satisfaction and business goals, they might not be adept at conveying the value of project management beyond efficiency, because their arguments are couched in iron triangle efficiency arguments.

Table 6.8. Exploratory Factor Analysis for the Very Successful Selling Model

Factor	Items	Items from Survey
1 Executive Framing	8_1	Senior executive interested in project management when the competition is doing better
	9_5	Successful approach—seller is trustworthy
	10_3	Present project management as a solution to a specific problem
	11_2	Use emotional, dramatic, or novel terms (urgent, failure, crisis)
	11_5	Describe project management using executive language
	11_7	Describe project management using supporting evidence, facts to justify value
2 PM Framing	7_3	Effective selling of project management involves project management staff
	10_4	Frame project management as uncovering issues, identifying solutions
	10_5	Frame project management as technique to achieve company mission or goals
3 Alignment	3_1	Project management is aligned with company's operational/business goals
	3_2	Project management is aligned with company's strategic goals
4 Iron Triangle	4_2	Projects at firm are completed on schedule
	4_3	Projects at firm are completed on budget
	4_4	Projects at firm are completed within objectives (scope)
5 Resistance to Project Management	2_2	Selling project management is hard to do at our firm
	3_3	There is resistance to project management at our firm
6 Senior Management Expectations	2_4	Senior management approves adequate funding for project management
	2_6	Senior management expectations are attainable
7 Value Statements	6_3	Project management enhances customer satisfaction, profits, market share
	6_5	Project management helps firm compete better than competition

Figure 6.5 presents these factors in a visual format to more readily show the relationship between the selling context, arguments, and processes.

Very unsuccessful sellers identify realistic senior management expectations and resistance to project management as the predominant contextual issues in their situation. This information reflects perhaps their focus on the environmental context within which they are attempting the sales process.

They also identified a hodgepodge of arguments for selling project management to senior executives, including executive language, alignment, iron triangle, and value statements. The major problem appears to lie in how they emphasize these factors in the selling arguments. In particular, these individuals were most likely to use *emotional, dramatic, or novel terms* to frame project management arguments.

More strikingly perhaps, *they made no mention of processes used to sell project management.* It seems that this group was relatively familiar with important benefit statements, with respect to project management, but almost wholly unfamiliar with the processes involved in selling issues to senior executives at a strategic level.

Figure 6.5. Very Unsuccessful Selling Model (19)

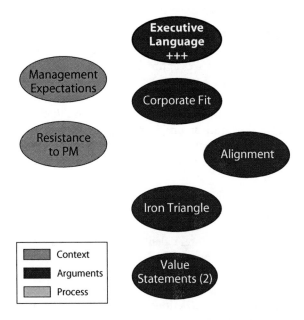

Overall, it appears that the very unsuccessful sellers use some approaches that the very successful project personnel and consultants did not, where the main difference lies in the inability of unsuccessful sellers to know how to effectively convey the importance and interrelationships among important factors. At the same time, many of the factors that the very successful models include are absent from the VERY UNSUCCESSFUL SELLING MODEL, particularly process-related factors. This result gives us some base-level knowledge about the most common contexts and arguments in which those selling project management are not successful.

What Convinces Senior Executives to Invest in Project Management?

Senior executives responded to questions about the process, arguments, and context of the buyer-seller relationship where project management is successfully sold to them. The demographics for the senior executive sample are presented in the next section, followed by a discussion of the factors identified in building the SENIOR EXECUTIVE MODEL.

Demographics

Some of the noteworthy descriptors of our senior executive sample are as follows:

- One hundred and forty-five are over forty (76.3 percent).

- One hundred and fifty-six are male (82.1 percent) and thirty-two are female (16.8 percent).

- One hundred and fourteen (60 percent) are from Canada and forty-eight (25.3 percent) are from the United States.

- Twenty-nine (15.2 percent) have less than five years of experience, and fifty-four (28.4 percent) had over sixteen years of experience.

- Ninety-six (50.5 percent) had only individual course education. In terms of level of education, forty-eight senior executives have at least an undergraduate degree (79 percent).

- Eighty senior executives (42.1 percent) belong to a project management association, and twenty-eight (14.7 percent) have a project management certification.

- Sixty-four (33.7 percent) spend over 50 percent of their time on project management, and one hundred and two (53.7 percent) expect to spend more time on project management in the future.

As compared to the general respondent demographics, the senior executive group represents an older population with a greater proportion of males in it. This group is more reflective of Canadian senior executives than the general respondent results. This demographic is likely due to the way we captured the senior executive respondents (using the CIO Canada mailing list that reflects a more Canadian-based senior executive population). In terms of project management training and general education, the senior executives in the sample have almost the same levels of project management education and had a slightly higher propensity to have some university-level education than the general sample. As expected, fewer senior executives spend the majority of their time on project management, but even among this set, the majority expect to spend more time on project management in the future. In terms of industries represented, size of organization in dollar sales, or employee numbers, the organizations these senior executives hail from had similar characteristics to the general sample.

SENIOR EXECUTIVE MODEL Findings (n = 190)

In the SENIOR EXECUTIVE MODEL, ten factors were identified in helping to explain how project management is successfully sold. Nine factors are statistically significant, only factor eight did not meet the rigorous 0.60 cut off. As described in the previous sections, each factor received a descriptive label. Table 6.9 shows the factors, corresponding item numbers, and items. Again, these factors, identified in the far left column of Table 6.9, are shown in order of importance, including: Value Statements (most important), Iron Triangle, Relationship, Resistance to Project Management, Executive Language, Competition, Corporate Fit, Organizational Tag Team, and Project Language (least important). The nine factors account for 54.0 percent of the variance, and the top three factors account for 27.3 percent of the variance. The KMO was 0.833, reflecting a very reliable factor model.

The **Value Statements** factor is the most important to senior executives. Not surprisingly, this group focuses on outcomes related to *efficiency and effectiveness values*, and arguments that show *how results can be measured* (either quantitatively or qualitatively) by using project management. Examples include *improved financial measures, staff growth and development, customer satisfaction, profits, market share, and non-financial measures of value*. These arguments related to the **Iron Triangle** factor, which is the second most important factor.

The third factor, which is also part of very effective selling processes, deals with the importance of an effective, credible relationship with the seller. The **Relationship** factor also points to the need for the seller to be *trustworthy*, and able to frame arguments that show the senior executive *how project management fits with the organization*, perhaps at a cultural or systemic level.

The fourth factor deals with a contextual variable—the **Resistance to Project Management** factor. Senior executive respondents reported significant resistance to protect management in their organizations, and this resistance affected the ability to sell project management in the organization.

The fifth factor highlights the importance of using executive language. The **Executive Language** factor points to the need for arguments to focus on *positive terms that emphasize simple, clear words related to success*, and that espouse the *long-term benefits of project management*. The very successful consultants tend to be very adept at shaping arguments around executive language (second most important factor for consultants) that catches senior management attention, whereas very successful project personnel focus more on the processes related to relationship building (second most important factor for project personnel) to spark interest in project management.

The sixth factor identifies competitive pressures as an important trigger to senior executive interest in project management. The **Competition** factor indicates that senior executives pay attention to arguments that *highlight previous successes* using project management, *point out what the competition is doing better*, and *highlight new business opportunities*. This finding suggests that senior executives look at competition-framed arguments about best practices, as well as identifying strategic opportunities from using project management. Neither very successful consultants, nor project personnel, use competition arguments. The unsuccessful sellers are using competitive-type arguments, couching them in emotional and dramatic terms that do not interest senior executives.

Table 6.9. Exploratory Factor Analysis for the Senior Executive Model

Factor	Items	Items from Survey
1 Value Statements	6_1	Project management contributes to improved financial measures
	6_2	Project management enhances staff growth and development
	6_3	Project management enhances customer satisfaction, profits, market share
	6_5	Project management helps firm compete better than competition
	6_6	Project management enhances firm's non-financial performance
2 Iron Triangle	4_2	Projects at firm are completed on schedule
	4_3	Projects at firm are completed on budget
	4_4	Projects at firm are completed within objectives (scope)
	4_1	Projects are managed with appropriate tools, techniques, and methodologies
	4_5	Projects are aligned with company's strategic plans
3 Relationship	9_4	Successful approach—seller is credible
	9_5	Successful approach—seller is trustworthy
	9_6	Successful approach—executive is supportive, approachable
	9_1	Successful approach—discuss how project management fits company's business
4 Resistance to Project Management	2_2	Selling project management is hard to do at our firm
	3_3	There is resistance to project management at our firm
5 Executive Language	11_3	Describe project management with positive words (success, savings)
	11_5	Describe project management using executive language
6 Competition	8_1	Executive interested in project management when the competition is doing better
	8_2	Senior executives interested in project management when they see new business opportunities
	8_4	Senior executives interested in project management when they hear about internal project successes
7 Corporate Fit	10_1	Frame project management as having a high payoff with few negative consequences
	10_5	Frame project management as technique to achieve company mission or goals
8		NOT SIGNIFICANT
9 Organizational Tag Team	7_1	Effective selling of project management involves middle managers
	7_2	Effective selling of project management involves PMO staff
	7_3	Effective selling of project management involves project management staff
10 Project Language	11_6	Describe project management by emphasizing detailed features, tools, techniques
	9_2	Perceived value: detailed technicalities, tools, features, processes

The seventh factor links the high payoffs of project management practices to its role as a technique to achieve the company mission; that is **Corporate Fit**. Neither the very successful sellers, nor the unsuccessful sellers, are using corporate fit selling arguments. This finding is very significant, because it points to a seller dimension that is relatively unexploited. Corporate fit arguments may be difficult to make because the payoffs, both in quantitative and qualitative evidence, are not well defined at this point in time within the project management community. Thus, sellers may have the most success by spinning selling arguments that include examples of previous successes achieved by using project management, particularly at the strategic level.

The ninth factor suggests that senior executives believe the sales process will be more effective when it involves middle management and project management roles. The **Organizational Tag Team** factor refers to project management staff, middle managers, and PMO staff. This finding is not consistent with beliefs that buying project management is primarily a senior management decision. The tag-team factor indicates that success in selling project management relates to the process of involving all levels of the organization. Both very successful groups focus on framing arguments in executive language and being inclusive in the sales process, in recognition of this finding perhaps.

The tenth factor, **Project Language**, points to the use of descriptions of project management tools and techniques, along with explaining their value, as being effective in the sales process. It seems that senior executives want to understand the details of the techniques and their corresponding value in a business sense. Unsuccessful sellers tend to shape arguments around features, but they overemphasize the "bells and whistles" of project management instead of tying these features to the long-term benefits of project management. Combined with placing less importance on value statements, this situation makes project management a tough sell. Conversely, very successful sellers (project personnel and consultants) couch value arguments in value statements that more clearly convey the benefits and link them to project management techniques and practices.

In summary, senior executives are first and foremost interested in business and project outcomes. The relationship with the seller is important and the business rationale, in terms of competitive pressures, high payoffs, and assistance in reaching corporate goals, when clearly tied together, catches senior executive attention. Lastly, senior executives expect an inclusive process that demonstrates how the tools and techniques provide value. Thus, they are more likely to entertain detailed, feature-driven arguments if clear ties are made to benefits.

Qualitative Analysis of Senior Executive Responses

In Phase II, the survey also collected qualitative data from senior executives. They responded to the open-ended question, "What three arguments or processes would be most influential in selling project management either to themselves or to their senior executive peers?" The data from this question provides rich and detailed information to cross-validate the quantitative data about what senior executives want answered in a project management sales pitch.

After analysis using qualitative software (Atlas), as described in Chapter 3, the themes, ideas, and issues strongly corroborated the findings from the factor analysis to further increase the confidence in the SENIOR EXECUTIVE MODEL.

First, most often (frequency of mention), senior executives want to know about the successes of project management in other organizations. They report wanting to hear about case studies and references to support case examples. This learning implies that those attempting to sell project management to senior executives need to *use reliable and well-referenced case study evidence* to demonstrate how project management helps organizations. Common references to "WACDAC" (words are cheap, deeds are clear) reinforced this need for factual and referential case examples. In short, sellers face a "show me and I will buy" situation. This finding fits with the importance placed on the **Corporate Fit** factor, as shown in the SENIOR EXECUTIVE MODEL. Senior executives need to *hear about past wins* using project management, and be able to see how they directly *relate to project success* in their organizations.

The next most frequently mentioned argument related to wanting to hear about the *benefits and value* of project management. Senior executives report being interested in a wide range of benefits including, but not limited to, the traditional *iron triangle-type benefits* of project management, with respect to better control of projects. Comments such as "on time, on budget, on scope," and "control, better control, and more control" often came up in mentioning project management benefits. However, as shown in the quantitative model, these arguments need to be tied more to the full spectrum of the value continuum, particularly with respect to customer satisfaction and value to staff growth and development.

As well, many senior executives commented on wanting to hear about the following kinds of specific benefits in sales arguments:

- Early risk identification

- Appropriate (measurement) metrics

- Improved communication

- Better scope identification

- Continuous improvement

- Staff development, retention, morale

- Repeatable results.

This list definitely suggests areas where even successful sellers can improve on the shaping of their arguments. In particular, sellers do not single out and sell the benefit of improved communication, for example, even though recent studies and empirical research points to communication as a critical part of managing projects (Delisle 2001).

Overall, senior executives want to hear about a full range of benefits from project management, and sellers need to extend these benefits to corporate goals and corporate objectives, not solely project goals. The following statements exemplify comments from the qualitative data.

> It would be important to us if it showed financial benefit, but more importantly if human resources, i.e., staff time, could be used more efficiently.

> Project staff will be directed, mentored, and motivated.

> Standards are measurable and provide early warning of problems … making improved decisions about trade-offs.

Similar to the first theme, a third theme in the data revealed that senior executives want to understand specifically what project management can bring to their organization. This theme emphasizes the need to bridge case studies and global benefit statements to the senior executives' own organization. It is important for senior executives to understand what project management can do in a global sense, as well as a showing how project management can specifically help their organization. This expectation includes an understanding of the business benefits of the explicit project management techniques, as well as an attempt (and commitment) to link project management to measurable organizational outcomes like return on investment (ROI) and goal attainment. This learning requires the sales person to link project management to the measurable strategic goals of the organization—not an easy task considering the difficulty in demonstrating payoffs discussed in the SENIOR EXECUTIVE MODEL.

The executives also emphasized wanting to know what project management would cost them, as an exploration of costs from the initial investment and ongoing investments. This particular finding shows a highly integrated understanding of project management as a strategic asset that is grown and developed over time. This recognition is in direct contrast to the decision to invest in crises-rife organizations, where project management is sold as a quick fix or "solution in a box." This evidence, as a whole, points to a knowing-gap in unsuccessful sellers who do not mention any process aspects of the selling process.

Key Considerations in Selling Project Management to Senior Executives

The following section provides a high-level summary of key comparisons between the GENERAL SELLING BASE MODEL, the Very Successful Selling Models (VERY SUCCESSFUL SELLING BASE MODEL, VERY SUCCESSFUL CONSULTANT MODEL, and VERY SUCCESSFUL PROJECT PERSONNEL MODEL), the VERY UNSUCCESSFUL SELLING MODEL, and the SENIOR EXECUTIVE MODEL. The first part of this section compares the common core contextual issues, arguments, and processes in successfully selling project management to all the processes and arguments identified in the GENERAL SELLING BASE MODEL. The second part of this section presents the highlights of the best practices from those sellers who report being very successful at selling project management. The final section briefly presents key differences in the unsuccessful selling group.

GENERAL SELLING BASE MODEL Findings

This GENERAL SELLING BASE MODEL reveals three contextual issues that are common across the study sample:

1. Competition: Attention to arguments that *highlight previous successes* using project management, *point out what the competition is doing better*, and *highlight new business opportunities*. Although this use of competition is a significant factor

identified by senior executives, even successful sellers do not seem to focus on competition-framed arguments as justification for investment in project management.

2. Crisis: The triggering of a crisis by an event (internal or external) often creates a context amenable to "trigger," or spark, interest in the sale of project management. Selling in this environment may be risky if the sales goal is to build a long-term relationship; because the crisis context complicates the implementation efforts enough so senior executive expectations are not met.

3. Accidental project management: The presence of the accidental project manager (does not have the formal training to manage strategic projects, yet is doing so often without increased incentives and compensation) results in accidental project management. This context may be so ingrained that it becomes part of an organization's culture.

Factors identified as important to successful selling include:

- Framing the project management investment in *senior executive terms* and as an executive decision. And, do so in such a way as to involve others who do project management in the organization. Although the final decision may belong to the senior executives, taking the time to build relationships with strategic advocates of project management within the organization (especially in the consultants case) may enable the sale.

- The content of the sales pitch revolves around a variety of *value statements* relating project management to corporate business outcomes and the *iron triangle* discussions *tied to project outcomes and practices.*

- In addition, successful sellers shape arguments to enable the *alignment of senior executive expectations and corporate goals* with project management outcomes.

The GENERAL SELLING BASE MODEL points to the key process consideration as it relates to deciding who is to be involved in the sales process. The process deems the involvement of both internal and external project management personnel as important to the sales process.

Very Successful Selling Practices

Those reporting the highest degrees of success in selling project management to senior executives allow for the generation of a refined and more focused model. The most common, or core, very successful selling contextual issues, arguments, and processes are briefly presented in the first part of the section. The remainder of the section presents the key differences between the very successful consultants and project personnel.

The two contextual issues important to this group include:

1. Resistance to project management
2. Realistic senior management expectations

The sales arguments by very successful sellers focus on *value statements*, followed by *iron triangle* discussions, and the use of both *executive language and executive framing* show the same trend as the common core selling arguments. The difference lay mostly in the "salespeople," that is, their ability to effectively tie together tactical and strategic value statements to demonstrate the benefits and payoffs that they are speaking about. As noted in the qualitative data analysis, there is room to improve, since senior executives want selling arguments to contain examples of previous successes and case studies/examples that they can relate to.

Successful selling processes of importance stress the need for developing a corporate fit and the selling relationship. The corporate fit issue relates directly to how well sellers tie tactical and strategic arguments throughout the sales cycle, so that these arguments are part of an ongoing effort toward establishing a lasting relationship between the seller and buyer. Effectively, very successful sellers are always being "tested," because the business context may change, and thus, the project management needs of an organization.

Very Successful Selling Practices—Consultants versus Project Personnel

Distinct differences are visible between the model created from the very successful project personnel data and that created from very successful consultant data.

Unique to the VERY SUCCESSFUL PROJECT PERSONNEL MODEL, they identify realistic *senior executive expectations* as the most important contextual factor. Thus, they lead sales discussions with arguments related to *iron triangle* outcomes and practices, framing them in *executive language*. However, they hone in on a smaller set of specific *value statements* about organizational development outcomes, rather than financial measures. Thus, more emphasis is on language, to gain a consensual understanding, rather than on *executive framing*.

In contrast, like the common core sellers, the VERY SUCCESSFUL CONSULTANT MODEL reports that *accidental project management* is the primary contextual issue. Very successful sellers pay attention to the accidental project manager phenomenon and the organization's competitive situation, as part of what Dutton (2001) calls "reading the wind."

They also shape selling arguments around a variety of *value statements*, using particular statements depending on the individual client and the timing. Next, they identified using *executive language* in framing *iron triangle* arguments, while aligning project management goals with corporate goals and executive expectations.

The number one process factor very successful consultants mention relates to *relationship* issues. These consultants pay attention to the relationship and political nature of the sales process, recognizing that the arguments they use and the way they are framed are actually parts of the entire sales process.

In addition, very successful consultants used *value statements* as processes to tie project management to a valuable corporate goal, as long as they are able to infer that project management will deliver such a benefit on its *own merits*. Otherwise, if these consultants indirectly or directly tie the sale of project management to themselves or success of the project management implementation, the pressure increases to meet senior management expectations that may be set too high or not managed well. The overall payoff to sellers is high if they are positively "branded" along with the project management being sold. On the downside, the risk is also high, particularly if senior management expectations are not aligned, or managed well.

Unsuccessful Selling Practices

In contrast to the other models discussed previously, the VERY UNSUCCESSFUL SELLING MODEL shows some interesting differences. Unsuccessful sellers do not appear to use what we treat as purely process-related factors. Rather, they identify the context of *realistic senior management expectations* and *resistance to project management* as a process part of the sales effort.

They also report using an unrelated mix or hodgepodge of sales arguments, mostly containing words that are important in *executive language*, in combination with *dramatic emotional terms*, which are unique to this model. They also report focusing less on shaping arguments around *value statements* that point out the quantitative benefit or effect on profits, market share, and competitive position. Ironically, these very arguments are likely the most difficult to justify or deliver.

Summary

Overall, it appears that the very unsuccessful project personnel/consultants used many approaches that the very successful project managers and consultants did not. Unsuccessful seller strategies are not as aligned with what senior executives seek, relative to the very successful groups. In contrast, the strategies used by the very successful groups are closely aligned with the *value statements*, in particular in the SENIOR EXECUTIVE MODEL, that manage senior management expectations about benefits.

In general, project personnel and consultants place different emphasis on, but commonly use, *executive language*, discussing the *corporate fit*, and present it as a *value proposition* when selling project management. However, they can improve by using language and arguments that convey, and more clearly articulate, the tie between project management and the business context in terms of results.

The point that senior executives are seeking business results is made in the second factor that they focus on—the project management *iron triangle*. Both the very successful project personnel and consultants use iron triangle arguments in their selling strategies. Senior executives are also primarily interested in, and pay attention to, project management when someone with whom they have a *relationship* based on credibility and trust presents it.

The overall finding from these models is that senior executives are mainly interested in information that presents key aspects of project management, as they tie into the business context of their particular organization, whether that means quantitative or qualitative results. They also want to hear about past successes, case studies, and examples with substantial evidence to help them see the payoffs for investing.

Best Practices

The next section provides a summary of the best practices—the most successful arguments, strategies, and processes. This section helps to draw out the best practice highlights from the data by comparing the selling approaches between the very successful groups and the unsuccessful group.

Most Successful Arguments

Successful selling arguments can be broken down into *triggers* and *descriptors*. All of the triggers and descriptors we tested against this sample were widely used by both those successful and unsuccessful in selling project management to senior executives. However, there are statistically significant differential trends between the level of use of these triggers and descriptors between successful versus unsuccessful project management "salespeople." This section presents the triggers and descriptors that were used more frequently by those reporting success in selling project management to senior executives.

First, and foremost, those successful in selling project management report the triggering of a crisis by an event (internal or external) as the most common way to trigger, or spark, interest in the successful sales of project management, and they did so statistically more often then those less successful. This result is what we would expect from our first phase results. It also points to the potential problems of implementing project management successfully under such circumstances. It may be that capitalizing on this most common and successful trigger may actually make the successful implementation and future sale of project management more difficult.

The second most common response was that new business opportunities trigger senior executives interest in hearing about new ways of working. This focus of senior executives on business opportunities and new ways of working apparently creates a fertile time to sell project management and involves tying it to the strategic direction of the organization in light of this new opportunity.

The third most common response of this group was to highlight early successes. This response equates building a strategy of "small wins," and using it to leverage further and future support for project management in the organization. As shown by the findings in the SENIOR EXECUTIVE MODEL and the qualitative model, sellers may improve arguments by tying together how project management performs, and successes in similar case studies or examples.

The fourth most common response of this group relates to stressing the competitive disadvantage the firm faces without investment in project management. However, these arguments are not couched in emotionally laden or dramatic terms, as with unsuccessful sellers. These respondents report that they describe project management in executive/financial terms, tying those arguments to long-term/strategic benefits, and combining it with detailed explanations of project management techniques. In other words, the best way to describe project management is to describe it as a management technique designed to improve the bottom line through supporting strategic initiatives, while at the same time educating the senior executives as to the details and executive outcomes of good project management.

In consideration of all the findings in this section, it is not surprising that using terms such as net present value, ROI, value, market share, and competitive advantage all help to interest senior executives. Finding that those reporting success in selling project management to senior executives also reported a higher incidence of using the details of the techniques in the cognitive arguments, was the opposite of what we thought we would find. However, it seems that senior executives are not necessarily turned off by project management techniques if they can be described in business language and tied to issues of interest to the senior executives.

Successful Strategies and Processes

The successful group also reported statistically different levels of support for a number of strategies and processes used to interest senior executives in project management. In general, successful sellers tried to use positive links to business and strategy, as opposed to fear-related crisis or emotional appeals. They also reported strategically targeting project management as a way to meet corporate and project goals, not just project outcomes, by linking project management to corporate strategies. Another successful strategy was to position project management as a solution to problems. This strategy in particular appears to be related to the crisis trigger for interest.

The successful group also tended to pay more attention to the people and political processes involved in selling. They reported involving more types of people in the sales process, including both internal project personnel and external consultants. This approach indicates that the successful sales may be a result of cross-organizational sales efforts. They consciously tied project management to company goals and built upon high credibility and trust to further establish relationships and build coalitions with supportive executives.

In general, two results stand out about the successful selling processes:

1. First, successful sellers focus on tying project management to corporate goals and objectives.
2. Second, successful sellers recognize the political nature and people-dependent processes necessary to interest senior executives in project management.

Conclusions

Selling project management to senior executives is an extremely complex issue, as evidenced in this report. As with many managerial issues facing organizations today, there is no "silver bullet" (that is, a single or one best answer that works in all cases). As we established, selling project management requires a careful assessment of the organization's strategic objectives, the project management situation, the executives involved, and the organizational climate or context.

While there is not one right answer, we make the following observations:

- Those selling project management need to be conversant in the language of business.

- Arguments that help educate senior executives about the realistic expectations for project management in their organizations are more successful in selling. Senior executives need to understand the importance of project management as it relates to their business objectives.

- The use of crisis/emotional terms in justifying expenditures on project management is viewed as unsuccessful in gaining senior executive attention and will likely cause a vicious circle of crisis-triggered involvement in trying to sell project management.

- Personal characteristics and credibility seem to be very important in building a selling relationship, which is important to the successes of very successful sellers of project management.

- Very successful selling efforts seem to require broad-based organizational support and coalitions of supporters, even though the final decision may still come from the senior executive.

- One of the glaring differences between the successful and unsuccessful models is in the width of the knowing-doing gap, evident in unsuccessful selling, that relates to the prioritization of and type of factors in the model. Unsuccessful sellers do pay attention to making similar selling arguments, but fail to recognize of the importance of the contextual issue, and fail to build relational-based processes.

Overall, the data reveals a common core of arguments, or processes and contextual factors underpinning successful project management selling. At the same time, no one best sales strategy should be applied across the board, because successful selling is sensitive to the instability of ever-changing client priorities and contexts, i.e., the global business climate. In essence, the approach that works for one seller may not work for another seller, in the present or, vice-versa, in future. As well, there are many different ways that salespeople themselves influence and shape the way project management is sold.

The next, and final, chapter provides some further insights into how to sell project management, highlights the important insights from this project, and points out areas to improve and future directions for research in this area.

CHAPTER 7

Insights and Future Research Directions

The difficulty in summarizing this research lay in its depth and breadth in covering two years of work. The project was an exploratory journey that began with a large number of questions to which we ambitiously sought answers. By the end of Phase I, we had generated several dozen more questions needing to be addressed to help fit the most intricate pieces of the selling puzzle together. Recognizing the magnitude of the task, we embarked on Phase II endeavoring to keep in mind the project objectives, the process, and the desired learning. Recognizing that research is an iterative process and that it can be very difficult to decide where it finishes, the following summarizes our current conclusions and insights on the project. Although each chapter in this report involves summary points and conclusions, the overall goal of this chapter is to link these points together to tell the story about why project management is a tough sell, and knowing this, how does one sell project management successfully. In doing so, we highlight the knowing-doing gaps that we believe are particularly salient.

Practical Insights

Phase I Insights

In Phase I, we asked the broad exploratory question, "Why is it difficult to sell project management to senior executives?" The focus of this phase was on exploring practitioner, consultant, and senior executive understandings of project management, and identifying any gaps that may exist in understanding the value of project management and the buying and selling of project management. As well, the exploration included looking at the process of selling project management and the interaction patterns between the buyer and seller.

The primary findings in Phase I revealed that:

- The perceived value of project management varied between the three groups addressed (project personnel, consultants, and senior executives). Many instances occur when the understanding of project management between buyers and sellers is not aligned in terms of it providing an efficiency-, effectiveness-, or innovation-type value.

- Senior executives recognize the importance of project management to their organization. However, they view it as of importance to a lower, tactical level of the organization. Thus, it stands to reason that project management only becomes a strategic or senior management issue when there is a crisis.

We developed several 2 x 2 matrix-type models to explain the process of selling project management and the challenges involved in linking selling arguments and processes to the value continuum (Chapter 4). The flow chart-type, major model coming from this work revealed a needs-based, decision-making process of problem recognition, information search, and the decision to act or deny the crisis that initially was triggered to elicit senior executive interest. The model identified the emergence of the "accidental project manager" as the result of not acting. The senior executive decision to act leads to different types of investments in project management that include developing it internally (strategic) or purchasing the services or project management tools (tactical).

Phase I findings led to recommendations based on a three-pronged approach, involving triggers, responses, and proof, that describe how to sell project management to senior executives. This framework highlights the standard marketing principles important in any selling process by examining the *triggers, responses, and proofs* that emerged as the major components of the selling project management research model. Albeit simplistic, this approach, based on the rich, in-depth qualitative interview data collected and analyzed with great care, generated important insights.

In general, *triggers* involve understanding what events or actions generate interest in senior executives in buying project management. *Responses* relate to reframing project management in terms of its benefits and its connection to values, relative to the senior executive's priorities, wherever they may be on the value continuum. This approach entails being able to state the value of project management in terms that support the business objective and corporate strategies. *Proofs* involve being able to demonstrate evidence to support the benefit claims. One way of doing this is to draw analogies about the impact project failures or successes have on the business strategy and discuss lessons learned. This process requires a tight alignment between business goals and project management that is also responsive to changes in the context of the sale. The entire framework may be reviewed in Chapter 4.

Phase II Insights

Phase II focused on answering questions like "What sales strategies are most effective (and which ones are not)?" and "What is the perceived value of project management?" as an important part in understanding why project management is a tough sell. The literature review of the marketing and sales, organizational theory, project management, and strategy, and findings and interpretation of selling gained from Phase I, formed a beginning for the underlying theory that helped to shape Phase II data collection. Phase II focused on examining the concepts about selling in more detail and from different angles to see if the pattern of themes could be validated on a generalizable scale. The results from Phase II show which of these patterns has the highest explanatory power in understanding how to sell project management with a high degree of statistical accuracy. The rigorous factor analysis allowed us to examine how much power the concepts of interest (independent variables) had in helping to explain the selling arguments, processes, and contexts. Furthermore, the analysis helped to cleanly separate the statistically significant groups of factors that formed the models with the most ability to explain the most common selling arguments, processes, and contexts. Finally, the effort resulted in the emergence of models that show the most successful and unsuccessful arguments, processes, and contexts involved in selling project management processes.

The amount and complexity of findings from Phase II is staggering. However, this report contains the key practical findings in order to make this report as useful as possible to the reader. At a high level, the findings indicate that:

- Senior executives recognize project management as having strategic, as well as tactical, value in their organizations. At the same time, there remains an average of 35 percent of all respondents who report not recognizing project management as having a strategic role to play.

- It appears that accidental project managers managing strategically important projects are not achieving the outcomes they expect, and are not using the appropriate project management tools and techniques.

- By analyzing the data by participant position, industry, and country, the outcome statistics show that strategically important projects are not meeting specifications, cost, or schedule expectations relatively consistently across these categories.

Considering Phase II findings and interpretations at a high level, selling arguments can be broken down into triggers and descriptors. All of the triggers and descriptors that were tested against the study sample were widely used by both those successful and unsuccessful in selling project management to senior executives. However, there are statistically significant different trends between the levels of successful versus unsuccessful project management salespeople.

This learning was in keeping with our Phase I recommendations involving the importance of triggers, responses, and proof in the sale of project management to senior executives. The Phase II data grouped into factors differently for the various models of analysis; the findings, with respect to these concepts, are comparable. The trigger, response, and proof framework from Phase I is clearly related to understanding how project management is used, particularly in understanding what arguments, processes, and contexts are commonly used in selling project management successfully, as revealed in Phase II data analysis.

Very Successful Arguments

Those respondents reporting being very successful in selling project management to senior executives use statistically different arguments and processes from those reporting being unsuccessful. It is important to review these differences to deduce how project management can be more successfully sold to senior executives. The following discussion explores the differences in what the very successful salespeople ultimately argued and did. Each of the five most successful triggers/descriptors is described in the following paragraphs.

First and foremost, Phase II findings reveal that those successful in selling project management report the presence of crisis as most significant in triggering the successful sale of project management, and those who sold under this condition did so statistically more often then those less successful. Although the trigger itself may be internal (CEO fired) or external (market crash), a crisis ensued and led to the sale of project management. This result corroborates findings from Phase I. Knowing this, the seller has to be aware of the potential problems of implementing project management successfully under such crisis circumstances. It may be that capitalizing on this, the most successful and common of triggers, may actually make the successful implementation and future sale of project management more difficult.

The second most common response in selling related to making innovative arguments about new business opportunities to trigger senior executive's interest in new ways of working. This type of occurrence is apparently a fertile time to sell project management by tying project management to the strategic direction of the organization, in light of this new opportunity.

The third most common response was for sellers to highlight early successes. This learning reflects building a strategy of "small wins," and using these wins to leverage further and future support for project management in the organization.

The fourth most common response sellers reported was to stress the potential corporate benefits achievable through successful implementation of project management. Respondents report describing project management in terms of potential senior executive/financial value, tying those arguments to long term/strategic benefits, and combining arguments with detailed explanations of project management techniques. In other words, the best way to describe project management is as a management technique designed to improve the bottom line, through supporting strategic initiatives, while at the same time educating the executives as to the details and executive outcomes of good project management.

It is not surprising that using terms such as net present value, return on investment, value, market share, and competitive advantage all help to interest senior executives. Those reporting being successful in selling project management to senior executives also reported a higher incidence of using the details of the techniques in the cognitive arguments, which was the opposite of what we thought we would find. It seems that senior executives are not necessarily turned off by the techniques, if they can be described in business language and tied to issues of interest to them.

The very successful sellers group also reported statistically different levels of support for a number of strategies and processes used to interest senior executives in project management. In general, they tried to use positive links to business and strategy, as opposed to fear-related, crisis, or emotional appeals. They also reported strategically targeting project management, by linking project management to corporate strategies, as a way to help senior executives in meeting corporate and project goals, and not just project outcomes.

Another very successful argument was to position project management as a solution to problems. This latter one, in particular, appears to be related to the Crisis Trigger factor. They also tended to pay more attention to the people and political processes involved in selling. They built upon high credibility, high trust, and established relationships with supportive senior executives to build coalitions.

The fifth most common response in selling related to making innovative arguments to position project management as a solution to problems—whatever they may be. They build upon high credibility, high trust, and established relationships with supportive senior executives to build or strengthen existing coalitions.

While very successful sellers present the air of tying project management to corporate goals and objectives by being politically astute, the sell relates mostly to stamping out a crisis or potentially flammable situation. These types of arguments may also create long-term problems of gaining re-entry to sell project management if organizations find that senior management expectations have not been met.

Conversely, successful arguments that build on the trust-credibility relationship with the buyer help sellers to establish themselves and/or project management as a brand or distinctive identity that promises value from project management. Branding helps the buyer and seller establish common value statements about the benefits of project management so that gaining entry for future sales may be more likely. The actions of professional organizations, such as the Project Management Institute (PMI®), help to create a project management brand that may enhance the credibility of project managers over time.

Very Successful Processes

As mentioned earlier, there are no silver bullets to successfully sell project management. However, there are guidelines that effective salespeople can employ to bring project management to the attention of senior executives. Selling project management to senior executives is like being able to "read the wind" (Dutton et al. 1997). Selling moves that matter (arguments, processes, and contexts) is framed as a blend of how the material is packaged (presented and bundled), who is involved, and the process of selling it.

Suggestions About How to Sell Project Management to Senior Executives

Examination and interpretation of the data from Phase I and II, creation of models, a critical review of the literature, and discussing selling frameworks as they emerge in the research, all contributed to help us bind together what may be seen as the very early foundations for theoretical ideas about the stages in selling project management to senior executives. In short, the selling journey may best be described as a cycle of **Planning the Initiative**, **Reading the Organizational Environment**, and **Framing the Moves That Matter**. This work builds explicitly on Dutton and her associates' work (1988; 1993; 1997; 2000) on selling strategic issues to senior management.

Planning the Initiative

Given the intended audience for this report, it is unlikely that we need to belabor this topic. The key is to recognize that selling project management to senior executives is not a simple matter of coming up with the most important value statements to present to management. Like any wicked problem, it is not that simple, the seller needs to have an organized approach to undertaking this important exercise. In particular, project managers must get beyond their own knowing-doing gap and apply the basics of project initiation to this endeavor. In particular, careful attention to some standard project management activities will improve a seller's chance of successfully selling project management to senior executives.

- Identify the stakeholders.
- Plan the project.
- Identify the risks.
- Work the plan.
- Adjust as necessary.

As with any project, dangerous or wicked problems may become evident later on in the sales cycle if expectations are not set and understood on both the buyer's and seller's part. Planning efforts should include flexible stakeholder strategies in the plan for how to manage buyer-seller expectations, with respect to understanding success criteria and their relationship to project outcomes in terms of foundation- and/or innovative-type values.

Reading the Organizational Environment

Recognizing the need to plan the selling initiative does not identify how to assess the organizational context. Over the last ten years, organizational theory, and particularly the work by Dutton and her associates on strategic issues, provides some

Table 7.1. Relational, Normative, and Strategic Context Assessing Questions (adapted from Dutton et al. 1997)

Relational Questions	Normative Questions	Strategic Questions
• Who will be affected by the issue? • Who has experience with project management? • Who cares? • What groups can advocate for or against? • Who does this threaten? • Who has decision-making authority? • Who has power to help or hinder? • When will people be ready to listen?	• What kinds of data do people use? • How is the data presented? • How are arguments made against an issue? • What kinds of protocols are followed? • What kinds of meetings are legitimate decision formats? • How much time does it take to sell an issue? • Have similar issues been sold or failed in the near past?	• What are the organization's goals? • How does the organization plan to achieve its goals? • What are the critical strategic issues for top management? • What is the broader competitive context?

solid advice on how to do this. This research makes a solid argument for the importance of anticipating underlying interests or, metaphorically speaking, "reading the wind" to determine the best track to take to reach selling/buying objectives. If you wish to be successful in selling project management to senior executives, you must pay attention to the context of the sale of project management.

Dutton et al. (1997) provide questions to help guide managers in selling strategic issues to senior management. We believe these same questions will be extremely valuable in the project management context. Table 7.1 presents a slightly simplified list of the questions they found to be important in their study.

By paying attention to these questions, sellers can more accurately assess the business context within which they are operating. This analysis will help you identify the appropriate actions to take to manage senior management expectations along the journey of selling project management. Although the results from Phase II show that successful salespeople do pay attention to the context, they are only focusing on some of these questions and not gathering a comprehensive view of the context. Thus, sellers' focus may be influenced by the context data they do assess, leaving them in a reactive position of falling into the old habits of "crisis selling." By paying attention to more of these questions, the seller can choose to actively "read the wind," which will prepare him or her to recognize and actively influence, and create the kind of context that generates the long-term selling relationship. Thus, with diligent attention to the relational, normative, and strategic aspects of the context, and being able to assess which ones are important at any time in the sales cycle, the seller creates a positive context within which to sell project management.

Framing the Moves That Matter

Having identified the sales context and the stakeholders and risks important to selling project management, the final step is to decide on appropriate arguments and tactics to use to raise the issue with senior executives. Again, the study results support the work of Dutton et al. (2001) in the area of selling strategic issues.

Specifically, sellers who focus on actions that matter pay attention to packaging selling arguments in terms relating to the logic of the business plan. Sellers also bundle project management as an integral part of the goals or issues of importance in the organization. As indicated in the models in Chapter 5, sellers must involve a wide range of internal and external project management people in formal and informal ways throughout the organization. Concentrating the sales efforts on an exclusive core group and distributing information through formal channels may be less effective.

Finally, any attempt to sell project management to senior executives must consider the appropriate processes. Consideration must be given to the formality, type of up-front preparation required, and timing of the approach. The process is interlinked with the context in many respects, so reading the environment and framing the actions that matter are essentially *iterative* and *ongoing* parts of the sales cycle.

Overall, successful salespeople do most of these things, whereas unsuccessful salespeople seem more inclined to ignore the involvement and process tactics. In particular, issues of timing related to crisis need to be given very careful consideration to avoid the downside risk inherent in capitalizing on an opportunity created when a the vulnerable part of an organization "snaps" and triggers an internal crisis.

In general, very successful project personnel and consultants place different emphasis on, but commonly use, executive language, discussing the corporate fit, and presenting it as a value proposition when selling project management. In addition, it appears that there are some selling practices that we can identify as unsuccessful. The very unsuccessful project personnel and consultants used many approaches that the very successful project personnel and consultants did not. For instance, unsuccessful seller strategies are not as aligned with what senior executives seek, relative to the very successful groups.

There does not appear to be one best sales strategy that should be applied across the board, because successful selling is sensitive to the instability of ever-changing client priorities and contexts, such as the global business climate. In essence, the approach that works for one seller may not work for another seller. As well, there are many different ways that salespeople themselves influence and shape the way project management is sold.

Practical Guidelines

While there do not appear to be any silver bullets or universal truths to successfully selling project management to senior executives, there are guidelines that effective salespeople can employ to bring project management to the attention of senior executives and get them on the same side. The following suggestions are made for those interested in getting senior executives on the same side.

- Understand an organization's key business priorities, and discuss project management in the context of measurable quantitative outcomes, as well as effectiveness outcomes.

- Explain project management in terms of the iron triangle (time, cost, and scope), but do not overemphasize project language (tools and techniques). Tie the tools to the business.

- Ensure that you, as a seller, have a credible, effective, and professional relationship with the buyer. In selling the services, it is less important to involve people at certain levels of project management within the organization—it is more important to focus on building a common understanding using executive language to ensure effectiveness of the relationship between buyer and seller.

- Understand how project management fits the organization in terms of operational and strategic goals, and discuss it in those contexts that make sense. The seller has to be sensitive to, and aware of, the possibility of switching gears in midstream of the selling relationship should the context internally or externally shift significantly.

- Do not use dramatic or emotional terms (e.g., the silver bullet, huge failure, or gigantic problems)—they do not seem to work. Very unsuccessful project personnel and consultants use this strategy.

- Do no fixate on references to competition within the industry—they do not appear to be a key factor causing senior executives to pay attention to project management. These arguments can also become entangled with the use of dramatic and emotional terms. Senior executives seem focused on the results they can achieve by using project management within the firm.

- Do not second-guess what senior executives are thinking about. The seller's views on senior executive expectations being realistic and attainable do not seem to matter. Selling arguments that challenge the realism of senior executive expectations were not a highly effective factor for the very successful project personnel or consultants.

- Focus on tying project management to corporate goals and objectives, and recognize the political nature and people-dependent processes necessary to interest senior executives in this management technique.

- Branding around project management appears to help the buyer and seller establish common value statements about project management so that gaining entry for future sales may be easier.

In summary, those reporting being very successful in getting senior executives on the same side use moves that fit with what senior executives are seeking. They frame project management by relating it to business results and the iron triangle, and use executive language. They recognize the context as setting and managing realistic senior management expectations of project management, and creating or entering an environment that has little resistance to project management. These sellers tend to use arguments that highlight a variety of value statements about financial measures, staff growth, customer satisfaction, competition, and non-financial performance, and link them to issues/values of interest to the organization. Making the value statements also plays a bundling role in the sales process. They also use project management outcomes and practices as important sales arguments. Although very successful sellers' arguments are sensitive to project management as a senior executive decision, they frame it in positive business language that speaks to solving problems. In terms of process, very successful sellers focus on explaining the fit between project management and the corporation or organization. Ultimately, very successful sellers pay attention to the quality of the relationship and building that relationship. They may be more adept at shifting arguments as the business context changes over time, thus, creating lasting buyer-seller relations.

Research Contributions, Improvements, and Future Directions

Fundamentally, this research project is like many projects; it is a unique undertaking setting out to accomplish something that has never been attempted before. A great deal of learning takes place over the course of a two-year project. This final section is an attempt to provide information about lessons learned from this study for those interested in the research contributions and limitations of this particular study, or in the future research directions we see arising out of this study.

Contributions of the Research

Practically, the value of this research rests in its ability to capture the underlying reasons why project management benefits are difficult to sell to senior management. In answering this question, the research provides arguments about how the selling process works and recommendations about how to sell more effectively. The research also identifies the processes, arguments, and context that senior executives are mainly interested in as they deliberate an investment in project management.

The findings are important to internal advocates of project management, who often appear to have the most difficult time selling to their senior executives. Additionally, consultants and other project management experts benefit from these insights, because they earn a living selling project management to organizations.

At a research level, this study introduced concepts from organizational analysis and marketing to help expand project management research's theoretical base. There is merit in making the interdependencies explicit between disciplines associated with selling project management. We also contribute to the growing strategy literature on issues for selling to senior management by exploring a significant issue (project management) that is sold to senior executives across organizations and industries.

Empirically, this study is believed to have one of the largest number of survey respondents of any research in project management, to date. It generated interest from around the world and provides highly generalizable answers to the questions of interest. In addition, it provides an important starting database for additional empirical studies. In particular, having 1,868 responses to questions on the practice of project management in organizations, level of project management in an organization, level of training and experience, perceived value of project management, and project outcomes will allow us to continue with further research.

We know that project management is a young discipline in the process of theory construction and that this process can be protracted in any discipline (Chalmers 1999; Delisle 2001; DiMaggio 1995; Reynolds 1971; Shaw and Gaines 1995; Sutton and Staw 1995; Thomas 2000; Urli and Urli 2000; Weick 1995). Our study contributes to this process because it strives to develop an initial theoretical view on why is it difficult to sell project management to senior executives and how it is successfully sold to them.

Additionally, the research contributes to approaches and the methodological assumptions regarding electronic data collection methods, as current literature sources show a lack of consensus on what an acceptable response rate for comparable survey formats and research designs is (Dahlen 1998; Gray and Guppy 1999; Hill 1998).

This report makes theoretical, empirical, and practical contributions to several bodies of knowledge. We know that project management is in the theory construction phase, and that a theoretical perspective on selling the concept is emerging. In part, this report draws from the current body of literature in management and organizational theory, and in part, it is developing a facet of what that theory would look like.

From a theoretical perspective, this report has integrated literature from marketing and organizational theory (strategic issues and sense making) and presents in detail, the interrelated arguments, processes, and contexts used to sell project management. We welcome further dialogue and research on this topic, as theory development is an interactive process that builds on the contributions of many.

From an empirical perspective, this study is one of the largest project management studies of its kind, and one of the largest online research initiatives. We had an excellent response rate to Phase II and gathered both qualitative and quantitative data that further enriched our understanding of how project management is successfully sold to senior executives. We were able to explore the benefits and limitations of online research data collection. In the process of conducting the online study, we learned more about web-based research and its limitations (response rates). We were also able to share our learning with organizations that gave us access to their email lists. Internet-based research is an evolving process. Associations and organizations with distribution lists are learning more about confidentiality issues, random number generating of lists, and so forth. We were able to explore perspectives from a range of project personnel, consultants, and senior executives.

From a practical perspective, we did not find a silver bullet or one right way to sell project management. As our in-depth Chapter 6 indicates, it is a complex, interdependent process. We did find that while each selling experience is contextually situated and therefore unique, there are some ways to approach each individual context that improve the chances of successful sales.

We view our practical contribution in being able to heighten awareness on the challenges of selling project management at multiple levels—with senior executives, consultants, and project personnel. We believe that awareness of the issue is key to being able to address it. It is important to view selling in the situational context—who are the players, what is going on in the organization, what are the requirements, what are the business drivers, and so forth. These types of questions lend themselves to exploring the appropriate processes and arguments that fit the context. Each selling situation is unique … just as projects are.

In addition, we now have an instrument for assessing how project management is sold and purchased. With some refinements, other researchers can use the instrument to build on the theory of selling project management.

Areas to Improve

With two years of research experience in this project, we are able to reflect on what could have been done differently. In hindsight (and assuming less limited resources) this list includes:

- Conducting a pilot project (Phase I) with more participants, and in cities other than just one Canadian location (that is, Calgary).

- Soliciting more female participants in Phase I of the study.

- Finding a way to interest more senior executives not interested in project management to talk to us for this study.

- Finding a way to increase the American (and the rest of the world) executive response rate, likely by finding a similar, but more international, mailing list to that provided by CIO Canada.

- Asking fewer questions on the Phase II survey. The overall length of the instrument may have limited response rates. This issue is a matter of balance. We asked many questions in Phase II to get at the breadth and depth of the topic. As with any large-scale research study, investigators are interested in collecting a good amount of data and balancing that with the budget, as well as the survey length.

- Asking more questions in the Phase II survey. We missed a few key data points that would have enhanced our study. For example, we could have asked questions about incentives to sell, to further differentiate consultants from project personnel. This lack of differentiation reflects yet another trade-off in the length of the instrument versus the response rate question noted previously. Future use of this instrument would need to address this issue.

- Tripling or quadrupling the time allotted for synthesis and write-up of the findings due to their overwhelming complexity, amount, and richness. As researchers well know, the synthesis and write-up are iterative partners. Thus, allotting more time for writing is appropriate in such as highly dense research topic.

Areas for Future Research

There are many areas of future research that stem from the questions that this research continually unearthed. First, and simplest to conduct, are follow-up studies using the existing data set to cross-validate the models, and continue building theory. In addition, there is significant room for answering similar or new questions of interest related to selling. In addition, new areas of research, identified from the work on this research project, will further our understanding of project management in new, innovative ways and different angles. These areas of future study are briefly presented in the following section.

Future Research on This Dataset

In terms of future research based on the same data file collected for this research project, many options come to mind. First, data from this study can be analyzed on the basis of a number of areas including gender, industry, country, education, the size of the organization, position within the firm, and so on. Analyses of this nature will also make important contributions to our understanding of project management's value in today's organizations. Examples of future empirical studies possible using this dataset include:

- Examination of the project management education levels and demands for project management education evidenced in this dataset.

- Identification and exploration of different variations in the perceptions of value and practices of project management among the three groups.

- Exploration of relationships between perceptions of the value of project management related to project management education and project success.

- Exploration of the accidental project manager concept, in terms of organizational support, education, training, and abilities to manage projects in relation to the abilities to sell and use project management.

Second, further analysis of this dataset can contribute to theory development in the field of organizational theory, particularly in organizational strategy and issues selling. The data collected for this project can be subjected to further statistical testing to help form a more solid bridge to work such as that Dutton and her associates have contributed. One of the fundamental limitations of her work on strategic issues in the field of organizational theory to date is that the research has all been conducted in single-organization, multiple-issue environments. In contrast, the research we conducted looks at a single important strategic issue called "selling project management to senior executives" across a wide variety of organizations. In this way, further analysis of this dataset has the potential to make further significant contributions.

Finally, this dataset is rich enough to serve as a foundation in testing other theoretical frameworks. One particularly important area for further analysis relates to studying different understandings or perceptions of project management, and finding out how perceptions are influenced by position, background, training, and so on. This work is needed to show the level of consensus in understanding what the profession often calls "commonly accepted" project management terms. The entire area of project management language, and the level of conceptual and terminology sharing between project management experts and practitioners, is relatively unexplored, yet vitally important to the area of project success. This work would build on the organizational literature on sense making, in general, and on earlier sense making findings and project success research by Delisle (2001) and Thomas (2000).

Future Research in Related Areas

One of the important questions continually raised in the course of this project was, "What is project management's link to strategic operations in firms?" This study did not address this issue directly. This research did serve to highlight the need to explore a related, yet different, perspective called the Resource Based View (RBV). This topic is currently being investigated as a critical topic area of one of this report's research associate's, Kam Jugdev, PhD dissertation. Her research examines the characteristics of project management and organizational practices (executive support) to develop this level of project management practice. Going beyond project management maturity models and exploring the knowledge-based assets within the firm will uncover the role of explicit and tacit knowledge. The ultimate goal of this study is to identify what project management looks like when it is recognized as a strategic asset, how it contributes to organizational strategy, and what support is necessary to achieve this goal (Jugdev 2002).

In biology, scientists around the world are working to crack the biochemical code for each chromosome to determine human characteristics. Similarly, strategy and economics researchers are working to unlock the code for competitive advantage creation (Boulton 2000). The components of the code for business value creation reside primarily within the firm and involve industry factors. Unlocking the business genome involves defining, grouping, and characterizing the component parts involved in developing a competitive advantage. Focus on this at a rigorous research level is needed because we believe that project management has the potential to be one of the important strategic assets contributing to competitive advantage in organizations today.

Another important question raised by many of our participants or audiences over the last two years relates to the question, "What is the quantitative value of an investment in project management?" This topic is not an issue this study even attempted to address. However, there is still a component of the senior executive market for whom nothing less than a quantitative valuation of project management's contribution to the bottom line will be sufficient to convince them to invest in project management. This segment may be relatively small, as the results show that senior executives tend to be cognizant that project management provides non-financial benefits, and recognize the difficulty of providing generalizable quantitative justification.

Nonetheless, many practitioners met through the course of this research are still fundamentally interested in answers to quantitative types of value questions. Another PMI-commissioned research project, which originated at the same time as this project, is focused on the quantitative value of project management, building on earlier work by Dr. William Ibbs (1997). This project was awarded to Dr. William Ibbs, was partially funded by PMI, and resulted in the publication of *Quantifying the Value of Project Management* (Ibbs and Reginato 2002). These two studies taken together will paint a fuller picture of the entire value continuum of importance and use in project management, versus what is perceived to be and currently used to measure the worth and success of a project.

Professionalization is one last area related to the value of project management in organizations, and ultimately to society, that is of interest as future research. There has been much debate over the last few years about the need for project management to be recognized officially as a profession (like law or engineering professions). PMI has explicitly identified the professionalization project as part of its operational mandate. While there are a small number of traditional and legally recognized professions, project management is likely to follow the path of what is called the new professions like nursing, social work, and teaching. Understanding the costs and implications of these professionalization efforts will further the development of concise value statements about the practice of project management; Dr. Janice Thomas and Dr. Bill Zwerman have begun such studies.

Final Words

In summary, a great deal of learning takes place over the course of a research project of this length and nature. Some of the challenges are inherent in the changes in data collection to electronic mediums, and some are related to the youth of project management research that is empirically grounded. There are a great many different ways to approach the issue of selling, some of which, in hindsight, may have been quite useful in helping to piece the selling puzzle together. Regardless, this project successfully accomplished its initial goals and made significant contributions to the theoretical and empirical development of the area of understanding the selling of project management. Within the limitations established within the body of the report, the conclusions and interpretations about selling apply. We sincerely hope that each reader of this book will find one or more pieces of learning that can be readily applied in their application of, or decisions about, project management.

Appendix A: Phase I Interview Instrument

1. What is project management?

2. If we asked you to brainstorm around the word project management—I say project management, what words jump to mind for you?

3. If I asked you to do the same thing about the value of project management, what words come to mind?

4. What skills and competencies do you expect from project managers?

5. What should project management accomplish for a company?

6. What are the key concerns driving your industry or your organization, in particular?

7. What role does project management play in this company?

8. What are the barriers to a successful project management experience?

9. Is project management a corporate tactic or a strategy in this company?

10. Where do you see the company going in the future? Do you have a vision of what it will be down the road, or is it an ongoing operation?

11. Is project management a corporate tactic or a strategy?

12. What's your vision of the role project management plays in this company?

13. What is your executive team's vision of project management in the organization?

14. When you've observed that, in terms of senior management resisting the value of project management, how might you counter those arguments?

15. How do you get the executives' attention around project management?

16. What was project management like when you came into the organization? Did you come into it at ground zero?

17. What did you do to build it?

18. What was project management like then?

19. What was the main reason you brought project management in?

20. What were one or two key turning points or events that influenced the implementation or the value of project management within this organization?

21. Did you have to convince anybody that this had to be a competency?

22. How do you buy project management services?

23. What experiences or events positively or negatively impacted your decisions to buy into it?

24. Was formal project training or education a part of developing your staff?

25. What was the most difficult part of the process?

26. What kind of arguments given to you from outside consultants would make you buy project management? What do you want to hear about project management?

27. If you were looking for a project manager, and these other firms where you have relationships didn't have someone available, how could someone come in and sell you project management?

28. What would you be looking for in someone who has credentials and some experience?

29. How would you evaluate that person?

30. Are there any corporate metrics that the company may have in place that you've been able to track to be able to quantify success?

31. What was the most difficult part of the process of implementing project management?

32. Did you face any resistance?

33. What performance measures do you use to gauge whether project management has been successfully implemented?

34. How do you build awareness of the value and benefits of project management internally?

35. In your opinion, why is project management a tough sell?

36. Given the topic of discussion for today and where we're going with our research project, are there any other ideas or concepts or things you want to discuss or bring to the table? Is there anything we should have asked you?

37. What is your position?

38. What's your background and training?

39. In what industries have you practiced project management?

40. What professional designations do you hold?

41. How many years of experience do you have?

42. How many years of work experience do you have as a project manager?

43. What is your level of education?

44. What age category do you fit in?

45. How much of your work experience has been traditional project team kind of experience? How many years have you spent on project teams?

46. What's the best way to contact you if we want to clarify something out of this interview?

47. Could you put a dollar figure on the upper end and then the average cost of projects you've managed?

Note that 30–35 of these questions were asked of each participant, depending on how in-depth they covered the previous questions.

Appendix B: Phase II Survey Instrument

Athabasca University Project Management Study

Welcome to the survey on project management being conducted by the Online Research Institute in Project Management of Athabasca University. The purpose of the survey is to gather data on the views of project managers, consultants, and senior executives on the challenges of selling project management either within a firm or to a firm. Some of the findings of this research will be published in a Project Management Institute (PMI®) book, in PMI periodicals, and will be presented at a PMI Symposium. The survey should take approximately 20 minutes to complete.

By "project management," we mean the disciplines, methodologies, processes, and standards applied to manage projects in the workplace. By "selling," we mean promoting and advocating project management to senior executives in an organized manner.

There is no cost associated with participating in this study and all participants who submit their email address at the end of the questionnaire before Monday, 26 March 2001 will be eligible to participate in a drawing for a color screen, Palm IIIc.

All of your responses will remain confidential. Your name and email address will only be used by SurveySite™ for this research and will not be used for any other purpose.

Ethics committee approval for this project was obtained, in accordance with the University of Calgary and Athabasca University Research Services regulations. Please contact K. Jugdev for further information at (403) 258-2513 or kjugdev@home.com. Answering this survey indicates that you have read the ethics information provided through this link and that you are giving your informed consent to participate.

Thank you for taking your time to complete our survey. Your opinion counts!

1. Please indicate the one category that BEST describes your role within your company, as it relates to buying or selling project management services.

   ○ I am a project manager and one of my roles is to sell project management to senior executives within my company.

   ○ I am a consultant and one of my roles is to sell project management to companies.

   ○ I am an executive within the senior management team at my company and one of my roles is to decide/participate in decisions related to buying (investing in) project management services.

   ○ None of these labels apply to any of my roles within my company. TERMINATE AND GO TO THANK YOU PAGE.

The first set of questions explores your experiences with the application of project management.

2. Please indicate your level of agreement or disagreement with the following statements describing your understanding of senior management's views on project management at your firm. If you are a CONSULTANT, please answer these questions as they apply to firms which you recently sold/tried to sell project management to.

	Strongly Disagree	Somewhat Disagree	Neither Agree nor Disagree	Somewhat Agree	Strongly Agree
	1	2	3	4	5
Selling project management to senior executives is an important issue in my organization.	○	○	○	○	○
Selling project management to senior executives is difficult to do in my organization.	○	○	○	○	○
Senior management understands the cost of unsuccessful projects.	○	○	○	○	○
Senior management has approved adequate funding to support project management.	○	○	○	○	○
Senior management's expectations of project management are realistic.	○	○	○	○	○
Senior management's expectations of project management are attainable.	○	○	○	○	○
Senior management understands that an investment in project management is an investment in my company's long-term success.	○	○	○	○	○

3. Please indicate your level of agreement or disagreement with the following statements describing the use of project management, as it pertains to your organization. If you are a CONSULTANT, please answer these questions as they apply to firms which you recently sold/tried to sell project management to.

	Strongly Disagree	Somewhat Disagree	Neither Agree nor Disagree	Somewhat Agree	Strongly Agree
	1	2	3	4	5
Project management is aligned with my company's operational (business) goals.	○	○	○	○	○
Project management is aligned with my company's strategic (long-term) goals.	○	○	○	○	○
There is resistance to project management at my company.	○	○	○	○	○
Project management is used in times of crises (e.g., reacting to emergencies, putting out fires).	○	○	○	○	○
Project management is used to increase the likelihood of delivering successful projects.	○	○	○	○	○
Those involved in making key project management decisions take into account the interactions between the organization's projects across the company.	○	○	○	○	○
The interpersonal (soft) side of project management is considered to be as important as the technical (hard) side of project management.	○	○	○	○	○

4. Please indicate your level of agreement or disagreement with the following statements describing projects that your organization conducts. If you are a CONSULTANT, please answer these questions as they apply to firms which you recently sold/tried to sell project management to.

	Strongly Disagree	Somewhat Disagree	Neither Agree nor Disagree	Somewhat Agree	Strongly Agree
	1	2	3	4	5
Projects are managed with appropriate tools, techniques, and methodologies.	O	O	O	O	O
Projects are consistently completed on schedule.	O	O	O	O	O
Projects are consistently completed on budget.	O	O	O	O	O
Projects are consistently completed within predetermined objectives.	O	O	O	O	O
Projects are usually aligned with my company's strategic plans.	O	O	O	O	O

5. Please indicate your level of agreement or disagreement with the following statements regarding project managers in your organization. If you are a CONSULTANT, please answer these questions as they apply to firms which you recently sold/tried to sell project management to.

	Strongly Disagree	Somewhat Disagree	Neither Agree nor Disagree	Somewhat Agree	Strongly Agree
	1	2	3	4	5
Typically, project managers have little or no formal training in project management.	O	O	O	O	O
People are assigned the title "project manager" without recognition in terms of promotions or pay increases.	O	O	O	O	O
Project management professional development or training is supported.	O	O	O	O	O
Project managers have the authority to do what is needed to manage projects properly.	O	O	O	O	O

6. Please indicate your level of agreement or disagreement with the following statements on the perceived value or benefits that project management provides your firm. If you are a CONSULTANT, please answer these questions as they apply to firms which you recently sold/tried to sell project management to.

	Strongly Disagree	Somewhat Disagree	Neither Agree nor Disagree	Somewhat Agree	Strongly Agree
	1	2	3	4	5
Project management contributes towards improving financial measures in areas such as: return on investments, net present value, sales growth, and cost reduction.	○	○	○	○	○
Project management enhances project staff growth and development (e.g., staff satisfaction, retention, training, productivity, motivation).	○	○	○	○	○
Project management enhances customer satisfaction (e.g., customer retention, customer profitability, market share).	○	○	○	○	○
Project management is a valued discipline like finance, engineering, or information systems.	○	○	○	○	○
Project management helps my firm perform better than the competition.	○	○	○	○	○
Project management enhances my firm's performance in non-financial ways (e.g., organizational effectiveness, knowledge, learning, intellectual capital, capabilities).	○	○	○	○	○

The next set of questions explores your experiences with selling (or being sold) project management. "Selling" is defined as "promoting and advocating for project management to senior executives in an organized manner."

7. If you are a PROJECT MANAGER or a CONSULTANT, please indicate your level of agreement or disagreement with the following statements related to individuals selling project management to senior executives. If you are an EXECUTIVE, please indicate your level of agreement or disagreement with the following statements as it relates to individuals selling project management to you.

	Strongly Disagree	Somewhat Disagree	Neither Agree nor Disagree	Somewhat Agree	Strongly Agree
	1	2	3	4	5
We were more effective in selling project management to senior executives when middle manager(s) were involved in the process.	O	O	O	O	O
We were more effective in selling project management to senior executives when project management office staff was involved in the process.	O	O	O	O	O
We were more effective in selling project management to senior executives when project manager(s) were involved in the process.	O	O	O	O	O
We were more effective in selling project management to senior executives when marketing or sales people external to the firm were involved in the process.	O	O	O	O	O
We were more effective in selling project management to senior executives when external consultant(s) to the firm were involved in the process.	O	O	O	O	O

8. Please indicate your level of agreement or disagreement with the following statements. "In my experience, senior executives are more interested in project management when …"

	Strongly Disagree	Somewhat Disagree	Neither Agree nor Disagree	Somewhat Agree	Strongly Agree
	1	2	3	4	5
"they hear that the competition is doing better than their own company."	O	O	O	O	O
"they see the potential for new business opportunities in the future."	O	O	O	O	O
"there is an internal project crisis or failure."	O	O	O	O	O
"they hear about earlier project successes at their company."	O	O	O	O	O

9. If you are a PROJECT MANAGER or a CONSULTANT, please indicate your level of agreement or disagreement with the following approaches and how they have helped you to sell project management to senior executives. If you are an EXECUTIVE, please indicate your level of agreement or disagreement with the following approaches and how they have helped to increase your interest in project management.

	Strongly Disagree	Somewhat Disagree	Neither Agree nor Disagree	Somewhat Agree	Strongly Agree
	1	2	3	4	5
We discussed how project management fit with the company's business.	○	○	○	○	○
We discussed the detailed technicalities of project management (e.g., tools, features, processes).	○	○	○	○	○
We had an existing business relationship.	○	○	○	○	○
The seller was seen as credible.	○	○	○	○	○
The seller was seen as trustworthy.	○	○	○	○	○
The executive was supportive and approachable.	○	○	○	○	○

10. If you are a PROJECT MANAGER or a CONSULTANT, please indicate your level of agreement or disagreement with the following ways of framing project management and how they have helped you to sell project management to executives. If you are an EXECUTIVE, please indicate your level of agreement or disagreement with the following ways of framing project management and how they have helped to increase your interest in project management.

	Strongly Disagree	Somewhat Disagree	Neither Agree nor Disagree	Somewhat Agree	Strongly Agree
	1	2	3	4	5
Project management was presented as having a high payoff with few negative consequences or negative returns for the company.	○	○	○	○	○
Project management was presented as an executive decision.	○	○	○	○	○
Project management was presented as a solution to a specific problem.	○	○	○	○	○
Project management was presented as a way of uncovering issues and identifying solutions to problems.	○	○	○	○	○
Project management was presented as a technique to help achieve the company mission or specific project goal.	○	○	○	○	○

11. If you are a PROJECT MANAGER or a CONSULTANT, please indicate your level of agreement or disagreement with the following ways of describing project management and how they have helped you to sell project management to senior executives. If you are an EXECUTIVE, please indicate your level of agreement or disagreement with the following ways of describing project management and how they have helped to increase your interest in project management.

	Strongly Disagree	Somewhat Disagree	Neither Agree nor Disagree	Somewhat Agree	Strongly Agree
	1	2	3	4	5
Using simple, clear language.	○	○	○	○	○
Using emotional, dramatic, or novel terms (e.g., words such as "urgent," "crisis," or "failure").	○	○	○	○	○
Using positive words such as success, opportunity, or savings.	○	○	○	○	○
Talking about the long-term benefits (e.g., organizational effectiveness or competitive advantage).	○	○	○	○	○
Using language senior executives can relate to (e.g., financial or economic terms when talking to a Chief Financial Officer).	○	○	○	○	○
Emphasizing the detailed features, tools, or techniques of project management.	○	○	○	○	○
Using supporting evidence or facts (prior successes) to justify the value of project management.	○	○	○	○	○

12. If you are a PROJECT MANAGER or a CONSULTANT, please indicate your level of agreement or disagreement with the following strategies and how they have helped you to sell project management to senior executives. If you are an EXECUTIVE, please indicate your level of agreement or disagreement with the following strategies and how they have helped to increase your interest in project management.

	Strongly Disagree	Somewhat Disagree	Neither Agree nor Disagree	Somewhat Agree	Strongly Agree
	1	2	3	4	5
Using informal communication practices, such as raising the idea with colleagues, managers, talking about it in hallways, and so on.	○	○	○	○	○
Project management being bundled with other initiatives being brought to senior management's attention.	○	○	○	○	○
Project management being linked to corporate goals and business objectives.	○	○	○	○	○
Project management's value being described as a way of fixing "specific points of pain" within a firm (e.g., an Achilles heel, weak spot, area of vulnerability).	○	○	○	○	○

IF "EXECUTIVE" AT QUESTION 1 SKIP TO QUESTION 15

13. Overall, please rate your level of success in selling project management to senior executives using the following scale:

Not at All Successful	Not Very Successful	Neither Successful nor Unsuccessful	Somewhat Successful	Very Successful
1	2	3	4	5
○	○	○	○	○

14. Before answering the next set of questions please provide us with the three practices or arguments you have found to be most effective in selling project management to senior executives.

1.

2.

3.

SKIP TO TEXT ABOVE QUESTION 16

15. Before answering the next set of questions please provide us with the three practices or arguments you have found to be most compelling when you have been asked to purchase project management.

1.

2.

3.

The next few questions explore the demand for project management education. Please answer each question as it applies to yourself (PROJECT MANAGERS and CONSULTANTS) or to your staff (EXECUTIVES).

16. In the near future, are you planning to participate in/send members of your staff to any education programs related to project management?

   ○ Yes

   ○ No (GO TO QUESTION 24)

   ○ Don't know (GO TO QUESTION 24)

   ○ No response (GO TO QUESTION 24)

17. When do you anticipate beginning these project management programs?

   ○ Already enrolled

   ○ Within the next 12 months

   ○ More than 12 months, but less than 2 years from now

   ○ 2 years or more from now

   ○ Don't know

18. What level of project management education are you primarily interested in for yourself/your project management staff?

   ○ Individual courses

   ○ Non-university affiliated certificate program (1–5 courses)

○ University affiliated certificate program (6–10 courses)

○ Professional certification program, such as Project Management Professional (PMP®)

○ Master's degree in project management (11+ courses)

○ Engineering Master's degree focusing on project management (11+ courses)

○ Business Master's degree focusing on project management (11+ courses)

○ Doctorate degree

19. How long are you willing to invest in this education?

○ 1 year part-time

○ 1 year full-time

○ 2 years part-time

○ 2 years full-time

○ 3 or more years part-time

○ 3 or more years full-time

○ Don't know

20. Would your organization be willing to contribute financially towards the cost of a project management education program?

○ Yes

○ No (GO TO QUESTION 22)

○ Don't know (GO TO QUESTION 22)

21. What percentage of the cost of a project management education do you anticipate your organization would cover?

○ Less than 25 percent

○ 26–50 percent

○ 51–75 percent

○ 76–100 percent

○ Don't know

22. Which one form of delivery would you be most interested in?

○ Worksite programs

○ Offsite programs

○ Online education

○ Combination of classroom and online

○ Traditional classroom on-campus university education

○ Other (specify)

23. What are the three main criteria you would use to select a project management education program? Please select only a maximum of three criteria.

○ Company approved

○ Consultant or instructor reputation

○ Cost

○ Distance

○ Experience of instructors

○ Online courses

○ Project Management Institute certification

○ Quality of instructors

○ School reputation

○ University affiliation

○ Other (specify)

24. Please indicate your level of agreement or disagreement with the following statements describing potential barriers to pursuing an education in project management.

	Strongly Disagree	Somewhat Disagree	Neither Agree nor Disagree	Somewhat Agree	Strongly Agree
	1	2	3	4	5
I have not been able to find a course or program that responds to my training needs.	○	○	○	○	○
Work demands do not allow me to take time off for professional development.	○	○	○	○	○
My personal obligations do not allow me to take time off for professional development.	○	○	○	○	○
The training courses that interest me are not available at a convenient time.	○	○	○	○	○
The training courses that interest me are not available in my area/region.	○	○	○	○	○

25. Please indicate your level of agreement with the following statements with respect to a proposed three-year, part-time, combined distance and on-site MBA in project management degree option.

	Strongly Disagree	Somewhat Disagree	Neither Agree nor Disagree	Somewhat Agree	Strongly Agree
	1	2	3	4	5
I am interested in taking (sending my staff to) such a program.	○	○	○	○	○
I would be willing to devote 10–20 hours per week (includes classroom time and time to complete assignments) to such a program.	○	○	○	○	○
I would be willing to pay approximately $30,000 CDN in total for the three-year program.	○	○	○	○	○
I would expect such a program to cover graduate level (as opposed to introductory level) project management topics.	○	○	○	○	○
I would be interested in the traditional MBA topics such as finance, marketing, human resource management, and strategy.	○	○	○	○	○
I would be interested in the "soft" project management topics such as managing expectations, negotiating, team development and management, leadership, and change management.	○	○	○	○	○
I would be interested in traditional project management courses on topics such as risk management, contracting, project control, and planning.	○	○	○	○	○

The final set of questions collects information about you and your organization, and will be used to compare groups of individuals who completed this survey. This information will be used for classification purposes only.

26. What is your age?
   - ○ 20 years of age or less
   - ○ 21–25 years of age
   - ○ 26–30 years of age
   - ○ 31–35 years of age
   - ○ 36–40 years of age
   - ○ 41–45 years of age
   - ○ 46–50 years of age
   - ○ 51–55 years of age
   - ○ 56–60 years of age
   - ○ More than 60 years of age

27. What is your gender?
   - ○ Female
   - ○ Male

28. In what country do you currently reside?

29. What is the highest level of education you have completed?
   - ○ Some high school
   - ○ Completed high school
   - ○ Some post-secondary education (college or university)
   - ○ College diploma/certificate
   - ○ Undergraduate degree (e.g., BA, BSc)
   - ○ Some post-graduate education
   - ○ Graduate degree (e.g., MA, MBA, MSc, Meng)
   - ○ Doctorate degree
   - ○ Other

30. What is the highest level of project management education you have completed?
   - ○ Individual courses
   - ○ Project management certificate
   - ○ Project Management Professional (PMP®) or equivalent certification
   - ○ Diploma in project management
   - ○ Graduate degree
   - ○ PhD
   - ○ I have not completed any project management education

31. During an average week, what percentage of your time do you spend on project management?

   ○ 0 percent

   ○ 1–25 percent

   ○ 26–50 percent

   ○ 51–75 percent

   ○ 76–100 percent

32. What is the likelihood that the percentage of time you spend on project management will increase in the future?

	Very Unlikely	Somewhat Unlikely	Neither Likely nor Unlikely	Somewhat Likely	Very Likely
	1	2	3	4	5
Likelihood of increasing percentage of time spent on project management in future.	○	○	○	○	○

33. How many years of project management experience do you have?

   ○ Less than 1 year

   ○ 1–5 years

   ○ 6–10 years

   ○ 11–15 years

   ○ 16–20 years

   ○ 21–25 years

   ○ More than 25 years

34. Do you belong to a professional project management organization (e.g., Project Management Institute, International Project Management Association)?

   ○ Yes

   ○ No

35. Do you hold a professional project management designation (e.g., Project Management Professional [PMP®] or International Project Management Association designation)?

   ○ Yes

   ○ No

36. What is the highest level of project responsibility you have attained?

   ○ Project sponsor (senior executive responsible for a portfolio, program, or project in terms of executive decisions and approvals)

   ○ Program manager (supervises project managers and is responsible for a portfolio of projects)

   ○ Project manager (supervises one or more project teams and is responsible for one or more projects)

○ Project/team leader (responsible for a subset of a project and reports to a project manager)

○ Project advisor (provides consulting services to the project staff or executive team)

○ Project controls officer (completes project control functions, e.g., schedules, budgets, other financial-related tasks)

○ Project assistant (works for a project team/lead and complete support functions as assigned)

○ Other (specify)

37. What is your organization's primary business activity?

○ Aerospace

○ Banking

○ Business services

○ Communication carriers

○ Computer manufacturers

○ Construction/Engineering

○ Consulting

○ Data processing services

○ Education

○ Financial/Accounting

○ Government

○ Insurance/Legal

○ Internet service provider

○ Manufacturing and processing

○ Marketing

○ Medical/Health care

○ Real estate

○ Research

○ Transportation

○ Wholesale/Retail/Distributing

○ Other (specify)

38. What were the overall gross sales (in USD) of your organization during 2000?

○ Less than $1million

○ $1million to just under $10 million

○ $10 million to just under $50 million

○ $50 million to just under $100 million

○ $100 million to just under $500 million

○ $500 million to just under $1 billion

○ $1 billion or more

○ Don't know

39. Overall, approximately how many people are employed by your organization? Please include full-time, part-time, and contract employees.

○ 100 or fewer

○ 101–250

○ 251–500

○ 501–1,000

○ 1,001–5,000

○ 5,001–10,000

○ 10,001–50,000

○ 50,001–100,000

○ More than 100,000

○ Don't know

Appendix C: Summary Tables of Phase II Survey Data

Levels of Agreement/Disagreement with Statements Related to Respondents' Experiences with Project Management

Within this section of the questionnaire, all respondents were asked to rate their level of agreement or disagreement with a series of statements related to their experiences with project management. An anchored, five-point scale was used throughout this section, where a rating of 1 = strongly disagree, 2 = somewhat disagree, 3 = neither agree nor disagree, 4 = somewhat agree, and a rating of 5 = strongly agree.

Level of Agreement/Disagreement with Statements Describing Respondents' Understanding of Senior Management's View of Project Management

The greatest proportion of respondents agree that "selling project management to senior executives is an important issue in my organization" (71 percent). Similar proportions agree that senior management "has attainable expectations," "understands the cost of unsuccessful projects," and "understands that an investment in project management is an investment in the company's long-term success" (62 percent, 60 percent, and 59 percent, respectively).

Table C.1. Level of Agreement/Disagreement with Statements Describing Respondents' Understanding of Senior Management's View of Project Management
(Question 2)

Base: Total Answering	Net Agree (4–5) (%)	Net Disagree (1–2) (%)	Mean
Selling project management to senior executives is an important issue in my organization.	71	14	3.9
Senior management's expectations of project management are attainable.	62	21	3.5
Senior management understands the cost of unsuccessful projects.	60	33	3.5
Senior management understands that an investment in project management is an investment in my company's long-term success.	59	28	3.4
Senior management's expectations of project management are realistic.	49	35	3.2
Selling project management to senior executives is difficult to do in my organization.	45	39	3.1
Senior management has approved adequate funding to support project management.	44	41	3.0

Level of Agreement/Disagreement with Statements Describing the Use of Project Management, as It Pertains to Respondents' Organizations

More than eight-in-ten (82 percent) agree that, "project management is used to increase the likelihood of delivering successful projects." While large numbers of respondents agree with the remaining statements within this section, in many instances, the proportion that disagrees exceeds 30 percent.

Table C.2. Level of Agreement/Disagreement with Statements Describing the Use of Project Management, as It Pertains to Respondents' Organizations
(Question 3)

Base: Total Answering	Net Agree (4–5) (%)	Net Disagree (1–2) (%)	Mean
Project management is used to increase the likelihood of delivering successful projects.	82	11	4.1
Project management is aligned with my company's operational (business) goals.	59	25	3.5
Project management is aligned with my company's strategic (long-term) goals.	57	26	3.4
The interpersonal (soft) side of project management is considered to be as important as the technical (hard) side of project management.	53	35	3.3
Project management is used in times of crises (e.g., reacting to emergencies, putting out fires).	48	36	3.1
Those involved in making key project management decisions take into account the interactions between the organization's projects across the company.	43	44	3.0
There is resistance to project management at my company.	37	44	2.8

Level of Agreement/Disagreement with Statements Describing the Projects That Respondents' Organizations Conduct

While 60 percent of participants agree with the statement "projects are usually aligned with my company's strategic plans," 60 percent disagree that projects within their company are usually completed on schedule or on budget.

Table C.3. Level of Agreement/Disagreement with Statements Describing the Projects that Respondents' Organizations Conduct
(Question 4)

Base: Total Answering	Net Agree (4–5) (%)	Net Disagree (1–2) (%)	Mean
Projects are usually aligned with my company's strategic plans.	60	24	3.4
Projects are consistently completed within predetermined objectives.	39	47	2.8
Projects are managed with appropriate tools, techniques, and methodologies.	39	48	2.8
Projects are consistently completed on schedule.	26	60	2.5
Projects are consistently completed on budget.	23	60	2.4

Level of Agreement/Disagreement with Statements Regarding Project Managers in Respondents' Organizations

The majority of respondents believe that project managers receive inappropriate levels of recognition (compensation) (60 percent) and training (58 percent). Interestingly, 59 percent state that project management professional development or training is supported (within their organization). Fifty-one percent disagree that project managers have the authority to do what is needed to manage projects properly.

Table C.4. Level of Agreement/Disagreement with Statements Regarding Project Managers in Respondents' Organizations (Question 5)

Base: Total Answering	Net Agree (4–5) (%)	Net Disagree (1–2) (%)	Mean
People are assigned the title "project manager" without recognition in terms of promotions or pay increases.	60	24	3.5
Project management professional development or training is supported.	59	30	3.4
Typically, project managers have little or no formal training in project management.	58	31	3.4
Project managers have the authority to do what is needed to manage projects properly.	37	51	2.8

Level of Agreement/Disagreement with Statements on the *Perceived Value or Benefits* That Project Management Provides to Respondents' Firms

At least seven-in-ten participants believe that project management enhances customer satisfaction (73 percent) and that project management enhances their firm's performance in "non-financial" ways (71 percent). Two-thirds feel that project management contributes towards improving financial measures in their firm.

Table C.5. Level of Agreement/Disagreement with Statements on the *Perceived Value or Benefits* That Project Management Provides to Respondents' Firms (Question 6)

Base: Total Answering	Net Agree (4–5) (%)	Net Disagree (1–2) (%)	Mean
Project management enhances customer satisfaction (e.g., customer retention, customer profitability, market share).	73	11	4.0
Project management enhances my firm's performance in non-financial ways (e.g., organizational effectiveness, knowledge, learning, intellectual capital, capabilities).	71	12	3.8
Project management contributes towards improving financial measures in areas such as return on investments, net present value, sales growth, and cost reduction.	67	16	3.8
Project management helps my firm perform better than the competition.	64	12	3.8
Project management enhances project staff growth and development (e.g., staff satisfaction, retention, training, productivity, motivation).	63	18	3.7
Project management is a valued discipline like finance, engineering, or information systems.	48	38	3.2

Level of Agreement/Disagreement with Statements Related to Selling Project Management to Senior Executives

The majority of respondents believe that project management is most effectively sold to senior executives when project managers (67 percent), middle managers (57 percent), or external consultants (54 percent) are involved in the process.

Table C.6. Level of Agreement/Disagreement with Statements Related to Selling Project Management to Senior Executives (Question 7)

Base: Total Answering	Net Agree (4–5) (%)	Net Disagree (1–2) (%)	Mean
We were more effective in selling project management to senior executives when project manager(s) were involved in the process.	67	9	3.8
We were more effective in selling project management to senior executives when middle manager(s) were involved in the process.	57	14	3.5
We were more effective in selling project management to senior executives when external consultant(s) to the firm were involved in the process.	54	19	3.5
We were more effective in selling project management to senior executives when project management office staff was involved in the process.	47	15	3.4
We were more effective in selling project management to senior executives when marketing or sales people external to the firm were involved in the process.	27	32	2.9

Level of Agreement/Disagreement with Statements That Complete the Phrase: "In My Experience, Senior Executives Are More Interested in Project Management When …"

Three-quarters or more of participants agree that senior executives are more interested in project management when "there is an internal project crisis or failure" (77 percent) or when "they hear about earlier project successes at their company" (75 percent).

Table C.7. Level of Agreement/Disagreement with Statements That Complete the Phrase: "In My Experience, Senior Executives Are More Interested in Project Management When …" (Question 8)

Base: Total Answering	Net Agree (4–5) (%)	Net Disagree (1–2) (%)	Mean
"there is an internal project crisis or failure."	77	11	4.0
"they hear about earlier project successes at their company."	75	7	3.9
"they see the potential for new business opportunities in the future."	68	10	3.8
"they hear that the competition is doing better than their own company."	64	10	3.8

Level of Agreement/Disagreement with Statements Describing How Different Approaches Have Helped in Selling Project Management to Senior Executives

More than three-quarters of respondents agree with four of the six statements describing different approaches to selling project management to senior executives: "The executive was supportive and approachable," (79 percent); "The seller was seen as credible," (79 percent); "The seller was seen as trustworthy," (77 percent), and "We discussed how project management fits with the company's business" (76 percent).

Table C.8. Level of Agreement/Disagreement with Statements Describing How Different Approaches Have Helped in Selling Project Management to Senior Executives
(Question 9)

Base: Total Answering	Net Agree (4–5) (%)	Net Disagree (1–2) (%)	Mean
The executive was supportive and approachable.	79	5	4.1
The seller was seen as credible.	79	3	4.1
The seller was seen as trustworthy.	77	3	4.1
We discussed how project management fits with the company's business.	76	5	4.0
We had an existing business relationship.	66	6	3.8
We discussed the detailed technicalities of project management (e.g., tools, features, processes).	52	22	3.4

Level of Agreement/Disagreement with Statements Describing Ways of Framing Project Management in Order to Assist in Selling to Senior Executives

Eighty-five percent of participants agree that presenting project management as a "technique to help achieve the company mission or (to) reach a specific project goal" is helpful in selling project management to senior executives. High proportions (71 percent) also agree that presenting project management as a "way of uncovering issues and identifying solutions to problems" is helpful in selling project management to senior executives.

Table C.9. Level of Agreement/Disagreement with Statements Describing Ways of Framing Project Management in Order to Assist in Selling to Senior Executives
(Question 10)

Base: Total Answering	Net Agree (4–5) (%)	Net Disagree (1–2) (%)	Mean
Project management was presented as a technique to help achieve the company mission or reach a specific project goal.	85	4	4.2
Project management was presented as a way of uncovering issues and identifying solutions to problems.	71	11	3.8
Project management was presented as a solution to a specific problem.	64	14	3.7
Project management was presented as having a high payoff with few negative consequences or negative returns for the company.	59	15	3.6
Project management was presented as an executive decision.	53	18	3.5

Level of Agreement/Disagreement with Ways of Describing Project Management in Order to Assist in Selling to Senior Executives

The greatest proportion of respondents (87 percent) agree that using "simple, clear language" and "using supporting evidence or prior successes to justify the value of project management" are ways of describing project management that assist in selling the concept to senior executives. Conversely, large proportions of participants disagree that emphasizing "detailed features, tools, or techniques" or using "emotional, dramatic, or novel terms" are helpful ways of describing project management (30 percent and 43 percent respectively).

Table C.10. Level of Agreement/Disagreement with Ways of Describing Project Management in Order to Assist in Selling to Senior Executives
(Question 11)

Base: Total Answering	Net Agree (4–5) (%)	Net Disagree (1–2) (%)	Mean
Using simple, clear language.	87	3	4.3
Using supporting evidence or facts (prior successes) to justify the value of project management.	87	3	4.2
Using language senior executives can relate to (e.g., financial or economic terms when talking to a Chief Financial Officer).	82	3	4.2
Talking about the long-term benefits (e.g., organizational effectiveness or competitive advantage).	80	6	4.1
Using positive words such as "success," "opportunity," or "savings."	77	6	4.0
Emphasizing the detailed features, tools, or techniques of project management.	45	30	3.2
Using emotional, dramatic, or novel terms (e.g., words such as "urgent," "crisis," or "failure").	26	43	2.8

Level of Agreement/Disagreement with Statements Describing Strategies in Selling Project Management to Senior Executives

Linking project management to corporate goals and business objectives is perceived as the most effective strategy in selling project management to senior executives (85 percent).

Table C.11. Level of Agreement/Disagreement with Statements Describing Strategies in Selling Project Management to Senior Executives
(Question 12)

Base: Total Answering	Net Agree (4–5) (%)	Net Disagree (1–2) (%)	Mean
Project management being linked to corporate goals and business objectives.	85	4	4.2
Using informal communication practices, such as raising the idea with colleagues and managers, talking about it in hallways, and so on.	57	16	3.5
Project management's value being described as a way of fixing "specific points of pain" within a firm (e.g., an Achilles heel, weak spot, area of vulnerability).	55	20	3.5
Project management being bundled with other initiatives being brought to senior management's attention.	48	26	3.3

Perceived Overall Success in Selling Project Management to Senior Executives

Participants were asked to rate the perceived overall success of selling project management to senior executives on a five-point scale, where 1 = very unsuccessful, 2 = somewhat unsuccessful, 3 = neither successful nor unsuccessful, 4 = somewhat successful, and 5 = very successful.

Slightly more than three-quarters of the combined total of project managers and consultants (76 percent) believe that they have been successful in selling project management to senior executives.

Table C.12. Perceived Overall Success in Selling Project Management to Senior Executives
(Question 13)

Base: Project Managers and Consultants	Rating	Total (n = 1,441) (%)
Net: Successful	4–5	76
Very successful	5	13
Somewhat successful	4	62
Neither successful nor unsuccessful	3	13
Somewhat unsuccessful	2	9
Very unsuccessful	1	2
Net: Unsuccessful	1–2	11
Mean		3.8

Project Management Education

After providing feedback on their level of agreement or disagreement with the statements that focused on experiences with project management, all respondents were asked a series of questions related to project management.

Level of Project Management Education Completed

Greater than one-half of the respondents (54 percent) have taken individual project management courses. Similar proportions have a Project Management Professional (PMP®) or equivalent certification or have a project management certificate (18 percent and 14 percent, respectively).

Table C.13. Level of Project Management Education Completed
(Question 30)

Base: Total Answering	Total (n = 1,758) %
Individual courses	54
Project Management Professional (PMP®) or equivalent certification	18
Project management certificate	14
Graduate degree	3
Diploma in project management	2
PhD	< 1
I have not completed any project management education	8

Anticipated Participation in Project Management Education

Seventy-seven percent of respondents expect to participate in, or expect to send their staff to, education programs related to project management in the near future.

Table C.14. Anticipated Participation in Project Management Education (Question 16)

Base: Total Answering	Total (n = 1,867) (%)
Yes	77
No	9
Don't know	15

Anticipated Start of Project Management Education Program

Among those anticipating that they/their staff will be participating in project management education, 51 percent are currently enrolled in a program, while an additional 45 percent expect to be enrolled within the next twelve months.

Table C.15. Anticipated Start of Project Management Education Program (Question 17)

Base: Respondents Anticipating Participation in Project Management Education	Total (n = 1,416) (%)
Already enrolled	51
Within the next 12 months	45
More than 12 months, but less than 2 years from now	2
2 years or more from now	<1
Don't know	2

Types of Project Management Education

The greatest proportion of respondents are interested in professional certification programs (63 percent) and individual courses (56 percent).

Table C.16. Types of Project Management Education
(Question 18)

Base: Respondents Anticipating Participation in Project Management Education	Total (n = 1,418) (%)*
Professional certification program, such as Project Management Professional (PMP®)	63
Individual courses	56
University affiliated certificate program (6–10 courses)	30
Non-university affiliated certificate program (1–5 courses)	23
Master's degree in project management (11+ courses)	21
Business Master's degree focusing on project management (11+ courses)	11
Doctorate degree	5
Engineering Master's degree focusing on project management (11+ courses)	3

* Multiple responses permitted

Length of Time Willing to Invest in Project Management Education

Participants are willing to invest time in their project management education, but only on a part-time basis.

Table C.17. Length of Time Willing to Invest in Project Management Education
(Question 19)

Base: Respondents Anticipating Participation in Project Management Education	Total (n = 1,391) (%)
1 year part-time	22
1 year full-time	1
2 years part-time	23
2 years full-time	1
3 or more years part-time	28
3 or more years full-time	2
Don't know	21

Anticipated Willingness of Employer to Make Financial Contributions towards the Cost of Employees' Project Management Education

Sixty-five percent of respondents believe that their employer would be willing to contribute financially to the cost of a project management education program, while 25 percent are unsure.

Table C.18. Anticipated Willingness of Employer to Make Financial Contributions towards the Cost of Employees' Project Management Education
(Question 20)

Base: Respondents Anticipating Participation in Project Management Education	Total (n = 1,429) (%)
Yes	65
No	10
Don't know	25

Anticipated Percentage of the Cost of a Project Management Education That an Employer Would Cover

Close to seven-in-ten respondents (69 percent) expect that their employer would pay for more than 75 percent of the cost of a project management education.

Table C.19. Anticipated Percentage of the Cost of a Project Management Education That an Employer Would Cover
(Question 21)

Base: Respondents Anticipating Participation in Project Management Education and Who Expect Their Employer to Contribute Financially	Total (n = 897) (%)
Less than 25%	5
26–50%	9
51–75%	11
76–100%	69
Don't know	6

Form of Course Delivery Most Interested In

The greatest proportion of participants (40 percent) prefer a combination of classroom and online courses.

Table C.20. Form of Course Delivery Most Interested In (Question 22)

Base: Respondents Anticipating Participation in Project Management Education	Total (n = 1,412) (%)
Combination of classroom and online	40
Offsite programs	19
Online education	17
Worksite programs	16
Traditional classroom on-campus university education	6
Other	2

Main Criteria Used to Select a Project Management Education Program

Nearly two-thirds of respondents (65 percent) stated that one of the main criteria that they would use to select a project management education program would be Project Management Institute (PMI®) certification. Other important criteria included the cost (45 percent) and the quality of the instructors (37 percent).

Table C.21. Main Criteria Used to Select a Project Management Education Program (Question 23)

Base: Respondents Anticipating Participation in Project Management Education	Total (n = 1,410) (%)*
Project Management Institute (PMI®) certification	65
Cost	45
Quality of instructors	37
Company approved	32
Experience of instructors	28
Consultant or instructor reputation	19
Online courses	17
University affiliation	17
School reputation	14
Distance	13
Other	5

*A maximum of three responses permitted

Level of Agreement/Disagreement with Statements Describing Potential Barriers to Pursuing a Project Management Education

Similar to the previous section of this report, participants were asked to rate their level of agreement with the series of statements below using a fully anchored, five-point scale (i.e., a rating of 1 = strongly disagree, 2 = somewhat disagree, 3 = neither agree nor disagree, 4 = somewhat agree, and a rating of 5 = strongly agree).

Close to one-half (51 percent) agree that, "work demands do not allow me to take time off for professional development." In addition, more than one-third agree that "personal obligations" (35 percent), "lack of courses being available at a convenient time" (35 percent), and a "lack of courses available in the respondents' area/region" (34 percent) act as potential barriers to a project management education.

Table C.22. Level of Agreement/Disagreement with Statements Describing Potential Barriers to Pursuing a Project Management Education
(Question 24)

Base: Total Answering	Net Agree (4–5) (%)	Net Disagree (1–2) (%)	Mean
Work demands do not allow me to take time off for professional development.	51	36	3.2
My personal obligations do not allow me to take time off for professional development.	35	48	2.8
The training courses that interest me are not available at a convenient time.	35	39	2.9
The training courses that interest me are not available in my area/region.	34	47	2.8
I have not been able to find a course or program that responds to my training needs.	22	56	2.5

Level of Agreement/Disagreement with Statements Describing a Proposed MBA with a Project Management Degree Option

Respondents are most interested in a MBA program with a project management option that focuses on the "soft" side of project management (86 percent), that covers traditional project management project management topics (85 percent), and that is taught at a graduate level (81 percent). Fifty-three percent of individuals participating in this research would not be willing to pay $20,000 (USD), in total, for the proposed three-year program.

Table C.23. Level of Agreement/Disagreement with Statements Describing a Proposed MBA with a Project Management Degree Option
(Question 25)

Base: Total Answering	Net Agree (4–5) (%)	Net Disagree (1–2) (%)	Mean
I would be interested in the "soft" project management topics, such as managing expectations, negotiating, team development and management, leadership, and change management.	86	7	4.2
I would be interested in traditional project management courses on topics such as risk management, contracting, project control, and planning.	85	7	4.1
I would expect such a program to cover graduate level (as opposed to introductory level) project management topics.	81	7	4.1
I would be interested in the traditional MBA topics, such as finance, marketing, human resource management, and strategy.	60	23	3.5
I am interested in taking (sending my staff to) such a program.	53	19	3.4
I would be willing to devote 10–20 hours per week (includes classroom time and time to complete assignments) to such a program.	51	31	3.2
I would be willing to pay approximately $20,000 USD, in total, for the three-year program.	22	53	2.5

Project Management Demographics

Belong to a Professional Project Management Organization

Slightly more than one-half of participants (53 percent) belong to a project management organization.

Table C.24. Belong to a Professional Project Management Organization
(Question 34)

Base: Total Answering	Total (n = 1,828) %
Yes	53
No	48

Possess a Professional Project Management Designation

Close to one-in-five respondents (19 percent) hold a professional project management designation.

Table C.25. Possess a Professional Project Management Designation (Question 35)

Base: Total Answering	Total (n = 1,838) %
Yes	19
No	81

Years of Project Management Experience

The majority of participants (58 percent) have ten years or less project management experience.

Table C.26. Years of Project Management Experience (Question 33)

Base: Total Answering	Total (n = 1,836) %
Less than 1 year	4
1–5 years	27
6–10 years	28
11–15 years	19
16–20 years	12
21–25 years	6
More than 25 years	5

Current Position or Job Function

Close to four-in-ten survey participants are project managers (37 percent), while nearly two-in-ten are midlevel managers (19 percent).

Table C.27. Current Position or Job Function
(Question 41)

Base: Total Answering	Total (n = 1,839) %
Project manager (program manager/project advisor)	37
Midlevel manager (director/manager)	19
Consultant	13
Senior executive (CEO/CIO/president/VP/owner/general manager)	12
Information technology professional	10
Engineering professional	2
Educator	1
Other	6

Primary Business Activity

Consulting and information technology are the most frequently reported primary business activities of participants (17 percent and 16 percent, respectively).

Table C.28. Primary Business Activity
(Question 37)

Base: Total Answering	Total (n = 1,838) %
Consulting	17
Information technology	16
Government	9
Telecommunication carrier	6
Manufacturing and processing	5
Construction/Engineering	4
Banking	3
Computer manufacturer	3
Education	3
Financial/Accounting	3
Insurance/Legal	3
Aerospace	2
Business services	2
Medical/Health care	2
Oil & Gas	2
Transportation	2
Wholesale/Retail/Distributing	2
Automotive	1
Biotechnology & pharmaceuticals	1
Data processing services	1
Internet service provider	1
Marketing	1
Mining	< 1
Real estate	< 1
Research	< 1
Other	11

Percentage of Time Spent on Project Management

During and average week, 59 percent of respondents spend the majority of their time on project management-related activities.

Table C.29. Percentage of Time Spent on Project Management during an Average Week (Question 31)

Base: Total Answering	Total (n = 1,842) %
0%	1
1–25%	20
26–50%	19
51–75%	22
76–100%	37

Likelihood of Increasing the Time Spent on Project Management in the Future

Sixty-three percent of respondents expect that the time they spend on project management will increase in the future. At the same time, 17 percent state that it is neither likely nor unlikely that the time they spend on project management will increase, while 20 percent do not anticipate increasing the amount of time they spend on project management.

Table C.30. Likelihood of Increasing the Time Spent on Project Management in the Future (Question 32)

Base: Total Answering	Rating	Total (n = 1,836) %
Net: Likely	**4–5**	**63**
Very likely	5	33
Somewhat likely	4	30
Neither likely nor unlikely	3	17
Somewhat unlikely	2	11
Very unlikely	1	9
Net: Not likely	**1–2**	**20**
Mean		**3.7**

Highest Level of Project Responsibility Attained

The highest level of project responsibility attained by the greatest proportion of survey participants is either project manager (39 percent) or program manager (32 percent).

Table C.31. Highest Level of Project Responsibility Attained (Question 36)

Base: Total Answering	Total (n = 1,840) %
Project manager (supervises one or more project teams and is responsible for one or more projects)	39
Program manager (supervises project managers and is responsible for a portfolio of projects)	32
Project sponsor (senior executive responsible for a portfolio, program, or project, in terms of executive decisions and approvals)	15
Project/team leader (responsible for a subset of a project and reports to a project manager)	8
Project advisor (provides consulting services to the project staff or executive team)	2
Project assistant (works for a project team/leads and completes support functions as assigned)	2
Project control officer (completes project control functions, e.g., schedules, budgets, other financial-related tasks)	1
Other	2

Area Worked in within Organization

The greatest proportion of respondents work in either the IT/Computers/Software area (40 percent) or the project management field (30 percent).

Table C.32. Area Worked in Within Organization (Question 42)

Base: Total Answering	Total (n = 1,838) %
IT/Computers/Software	40
Project management	30
Engineering/Architecture/Construction management	6
Marketing/Sales	5
Research and development	3
Contract management/Procurement	2
Financial/Legal	2
Manufacturing	1
Other	13

General Respondent Demographics

Role within Organization

The very first question in this survey was used to broadly identify respondents' roles within their organization, and to ensure that only individuals who identified themselves as either a consultant, senior executive, or project manager completed the questionnaire. Based on these broad definitions, more than one-half of respondents (53 percent) label themselves as project managers, while smaller proportions are either consultants or senior executives (26 percent and 20 percent, respectively).

Table C.33. Role Within Organization
(Question 1)

Base: Total Answering	Total (n = 1,867) %
Project manager	53
Consultant	26
Senior executive	20

Age

Seventy-one percent of respondents are between the ages of thirty-one and fifty.

Table C.34. Age
(Question 26)

Base: Total Answering	Total (n = 1,834) %
20 years of age or less	0
21–25 years of age	1
26–30 years of age	6
31–35 years of age	13
36–40 years of age	18
41–45 years of age	21
46–50 years of age	19
51–55 years of age	14
56–60 years of age	6
More than 60 years of age	2

Gender

Men outnumber women in this research by more than 2:1 (70 percent versus 30 percent).

Table C.35. Gender
(Question 27)

Base: Total Answering	Total (n = 1,821) %
Male	70
Female	30

Level of Education

Three-quarters of respondents hold at least one university undergraduate degree.

Table C.36. Level of Education
(Question 29)

Base: Total Answering	Total (n = 1,793) %
Some high school	<1
Completed high school	1
Some post-secondary education (college or university)	10
College diploma/certificate	13
Undergraduate degree (e.g., BA, BSc)	26
Some post-graduate education	16
Graduate degree (e.g., MA, MBA, MSc, MEng)	31
Doctorate degree	2
Other	1

Country in Which Respondent Currently Resides

The majority of participants live in either the United States (55 percent) or Canada (35 percent).

Table C.37. Country in Which Respondent Currently Resides
(Question 28)

Base: Total Answering	Total (n = 1,843) %*
United States	55
Canada	35
Australia	1
Brazil	1
India	1
United Kingdom	1

* Please refer to the data tables for countries reporting less than 1%

Overall Gross Sales (USD) in Organization During 2000

Organizational size, based on gross sales, varies widely. While 30 percent had sales of less than $50 million during the calendar year 2000, 29 percent had sales of $1 billion or more during the same period of time.

Table C.38. Overall Gross Sales (USD) in Organization During 2000 (Question 38)

Base: Total Answering	Total (n = 1,766) %
Less than $1 million	10
$1 million to just under $10 million	11
$10 million to just under $50 million	9
$50 million to just under $100 million	6
$100 million to just under $500 million	10
$500 million to just under $1 billion	8
$1 billion or more	29
Don't know	18

Number of Employees in Organization

Forty-two percent of respondents work in an organization with 1,000 or fewer employees, 26 percent work within firms who employ 1,001 to 10,000 people, and 30 percent work within firms that employ more than 10,000 people.

Table C.39. Number of Employees in Organization (Question 39)

Base: Total Answering	Total (n = 1,802) %
100 or fewer	20
101–250	7
251–500	7
501–1,000	8
1,001–5,000	17
5,001–10,000	9
10,001–50,000	15
50,001–100,000	7
More than 100,000	8
Don't know	3

Years Employed with Organization

The majority of respondents (57 percent) have been with their current employer for five years or less.

Table C.40. Years Employed with Organization
(Question 40)

Base: Total Answering	Total (n = 1,773) %
Less than one year	13
1–2 years	18
3–5 years	27
6–10 years	16
11–15 years	10
16–20 years	7
21–25 years	5
More than 25 years	4

Bibliography

ABT. 2000, May. Core competencies for project managers. ABT Corporation: Trends in Software Management. Available: http://www.tsepm.com/may00/art5.html [Accessed October 2000].

AIPM. 2000. National competency standards for project management. Available: http://www.dab.uts.edu.au/aipm/index.html [Accessed December 2000].

APM. 2001. Association for project management. Available: http://www.apm.org.uk/ac/cert.htm [Accessed 2001].

Bagozzi, R. P. 1984. A prospectus for theory construction in marketing. *Journal of Marketing* 48: 11–29.

Barney, J. B. 2001. *Gaining and Sustaining Competitive Advantage*, 2nd Ed. Upper Saddle River, New Jersey: Prentice Hall.

Barry, C. A. 1998, September. Choosing qualitative data analysis software: Atlas/ti and Nudist compared. Available: http://www.socresonline.org.uk/socresonline/3/3/4.html [Accessed June 2001].

Belassi, W., and O. I. Tukel. 1996. A new framework for determining critical success/failure factors in projects. *International Journal of Project Management* 14 (3): 141–152.

Bickman, L., and D. J. Rog, eds. 1998. *Handbook of Applied Social Research Methods*. Thousand Oaks, CA: Sage Publications.

Bistritz, S. J., A. Gardner, and J. E. Klompmaker. 1998. Selling to senior executives: Part II. *Marketing Management* 7 (3): 18–27.

Bistritz, S. J., A. Gardner, J. E. Klompmaker, and A. Plunkett, eds. 1999. *Selling to Senior Executives II: An Update: An Expanded Analysis of Two Studies Examining How Salespeople Establish Trust and Credibility with Senior Executives*. San Mateo, CA: Siebel Systems Inc.

Block, T. 1991. Selling Project Management to Senior Management—An EDS Experience. Paper presented at the Project Management Institute Seminars & Symposium in Dallas, Texas.

———. 1992. Selling Project Management to Senior Management—The Sequel. Paper presented at the Project Management Institute Seminars & Symposium in Pittsburgh, PA.

Boulton, R. E. S. 2000. A business model for the new economy. *The Journal of Business Strategy* 21 (4): 29–35.

Bounds, G. 1998. The last word on project management. *Institute of Industrial Engineers Solutions* 30 (11): 41–43.

Bryman, A. 2000. *Quantity and Quality in Social Research*. London: Routledge.

Cabanis, J. 1998. "Show me the money": A panel of experts dissects popular notions of measuring project management maturity. *PM Network* 12 (9): 53–60.

CCTA. 2000, December. Project management industry initiatives. Central Computer and Telecommunications Agency. Available: http://www.ccta.gov.uk/corporate/thisccta.htm [Accessed December 2000].

Chalmers, A. F. 1999. *What is This Thing Called Science?* 3rd Ed. Indianapolis: Hackett Publishing Company Inc.

CIPPM. 2001. Project management certification. Center for International Project and Program Management. Available: http://www.iol.ie/~mattewar/CIPPM/index.html [Accessed 2001].

Clarke, A. 1999. A practical use of key success factors to improve the effectiveness of project management. *International Journal of Project Management* 17 (3): 139–145.

Cleland, D. I. 1991. The age of project management. *Project Management Journal* 22 (1): 19–25.

Christensen, Clayton M., and David Sundahl. 2001. The Process of Building Theory. Working Paper 02-016. Harvard Business School Division of Research.

Compass. 2001. Making a case for the capability maturity model. Compass Fact Based Consulting. Available: http://www.compassmc.co.uk/UK/pubs/making.html [Accessed 2001].

Cooper, D. R., and C. W. Emory. 1995. *Business Research Methods*, 5th Ed. Chicago: Irwin.

Crawford, L. H. 1998. Standards for a Global Profession. Paper presented at the Project Management Institute 29th Annual Seminar & Symposium in Long Beach, California.

Cresswell, J. W. 1996. Research proposals: Presenting and justifying a qualitative study. In J. A. Maxwell (Ed.), *Qualitative Research Design: An Interactive Approach* (Vol. 41, pp. 99–137). Thousand Oaks, CA: Sage Publications.

Dahlen, M. 1998, January. Controlling the Uncontrollable towards the Perfect Web Sample. Paper presented at the ESOMAR Worldwide Internet Seminar and Exhibition in Paris, France.

Delisle, C. 2001. Success and Communication in Virtual Project Teams. Unpublished doctoral dissertation, University of Calgary, Calgary.

DiMaggio, P. J. 1995. Comments on "What theory is not." *Administrative Science Quarterly* 40 (3): 391–397.

Dinsmore, P. C. 1996. Toward Corporate Project Management. *PM Network* 10 (6): 10–13.

———. 1998. How grown-up is your organization? *PM Network* 12 (6): 24–26.

Dutton, J. E., and J. Webster. 1988. Patterns of interest around issues: The role of uncertainty and feasibility. *Academy of Management* 31 (3): 663–675.

Dutton, J. E., and S. J. Ashford. 1993. Selling issues to top management. *Academy of Management* 18 (3): 397–428.

Dutton, J. E., S. J. Ashford, Regina M. O'Neill, E. Hayes, and E. Wierba. 1997. Reading the wind: How middle managers assess the context for selling issues to top management. *Strategic Management Journal* 18 (5): 407–425.

Dutton, J. E., S. J. Ashford, R. M. O'Neill, and K. A. Lawrence. 2000. Moves that matter: Issue selling and organizational change. *Academy of Management*, In press: 1–25.

———. 2001. Moves that matter: Issue selling and organizational change. *Academy of Management Journal* 44 (4): 716–736.

EIU. 1999. Assessing the strategic value of information technology. Economist Intelligence Unit. Available: http://www.eiu.com [Accessed 2001].

ESI-International. 2001. ESI-International. Available: http://www.esi-intl.com/ [Accessed 2001].

Flick, U. 1998. *An Introduction to Qualitative Research*: Chapter 2: Theoretical positions. London: Sage Publications.

Gardner, A., and S. J. Bistritz. 1998. Selling to senior executives: Part I. *Marketing Management* 7 (2): 10–21.

Gardner, A., S. J. Bistritz, and J. E. Klompmaker. 1996. Selling to Executives: How Salespeople Establish Trust and Credibility with Senior Executives. Unpublished manuscript, Atlanta, Georgia.

Garson, G. D. 2002. PA 765 Statnotes: An online textbook. Available: http://www2.chass.ncsu.edu/garson/pa765/statnote.htm.

Glanville, R. 1997. Cybernetics and human knowing: Communication: Conversation. *Journal of Second Order Cybernetics and Cyber-Semiotics* 4 (1). Available: http://www.imprint.co.uk/CandHK/vol4/v4-1RG.htm.

Glaser, B. G., and A. L. Stauss. 1967. *The Discovery of Grounded Theory*. Chicago: Aldine.

Gray, G., and N. Guppy. 1999. *Successful Surveys: Research Methods and Practice*, 2nd Ed. Toronto, Canada: Harcourt Brace & Company.

Hair, J. F., R. E. Anderson, R. L. Tatham, and W. C. Black. 1998. *Multivariate Data Analysis*, 5th Ed. Upper Saddle River, New Jersey: Prentice Hall.

Hartman, F. T. 2000. *Don't Park Your Brain Outside: A Practical Guide to Improving Shareholder Value with SMART Project Management*. Newtown Square, PA: Project Management Institute.

Hartman, F. T., and G. Skulmoski. 1998. Project management maturity. *Project Management* 4 (1): 74–78.

Heinrichs, L. 2000, March. Sound-bite selling: communicating your value. *VARBusiness*.

Hill, R. 1998. What sample size is "enough" in internet survey research? *Interpersonal Computing and Technology: An Electronic Journal for the 21st Century* 6 (3–4): 1–11.

Ibbs, C. W., and Y. H. Kwak. 1997. Measuring project management's return on investment. *PM Network* 11 (11): 36–38.

———. 1998. Benchmarking project management organizations. *PM Network* 12 (2): 49–53.

———. 2000. Assessing project management maturity. *Project Management Journal* 31 (1): 32–43.

Ibbs, C. W., and Justin Reginato. (2002). *Quantifying the Value of Project Management.* Newtown Square, PA: Project Management Institute.

IPMA. 2000. IPMA Certification. Available: http://www.ipma.ch/certification.html [Accessed December 2000].

Jacobs, P. 1999. Recovering from project failure. *Infoworld Publications Inc.* 21 (39): 103–107.

Jugdev, K. 2002. Exploring the Potential of Project Management as a Strategic Asset through the Resource Based View Lens (Work in progress). Unpublished PhD Dissertation, University of Calgary, Calgary.

Jugdev, K., and F. Hartman. 1998, July. Leadership Fears and Frustrations in Project Management. Paper presented at the 3rd International Research Network on Organizing by Projects Conference (IRNOP III) in Calgary, Alberta, Canada.

Kerzner, H. 1987. In search of excellence in project management. *Journal of Systems Management* 38 (2): 30–40.

———. 2001. *Project Management: A Systems Approach to Planning, Scheduling, and Controlling,* 7th Ed. New York: John Wiley & Sons Inc.

King, J. 1994. Political maneuvers. *Computerworld* 28 (18): 91–95.

———. (1996). Say it ain't so, Joe. *Computerworld* 30 (50): 3, 78.

KPMG. 1997, 2002. What went wrong? Unsuccessful information technology projects. Available: http://audit.kpmg.ca/vl/surveys/it_wrong.htm.

Lesser, E. L., ed. 2000. *Knowledge and Social Capital: Foundations and Applications,* 1st Ed., Vol. 1. Boston: Butterworth & Heinemann.

Lim, C. S., and M. Z. Mohamed. 1999. Criteria of project success: An exploratory re-examination. *International Journal of Project Management* 17 (4): 243–248.

Lubianiker, S., and M. Schwartz. 2001. PMA 2000. Leshem-Nituv Engineers. Available: http://WWW.leshem.co.il/products/main1.html [Accessed 2001].

Lyles, M. A. 1987. Defining strategic problems: Subjective criteria of executives. *Organization Studies* 8: 263–280.

Macdonald, E., and B. Sharp. 1996. *Brand Awareness Effects on Consumer Decision-Making for a Common, Repeat Purchase Product: A Replication, Southern Marketing—Theory and Applications.* University of South Australia: Adelaide.

Marchetti, M. 1997. Whatever it takes. *Sales and Marketing Management* 149 (13): 28–38.

Marcolin, B. 2001. Management 783 course: Research methods. In University of Calgary (Ed.). Calgary.

Mason, J. 1998. *Qualitative Research.* London: Sage Publications.

Maxwell, J. A. 1996. *Qualitative Research Design* (Vol. 41). Thousand Oaks, CA: Sage Publications.

McElroy, W. 1996. Implementing strategic change through projects. *International Journal of Project Management* 14 (6).

McLaughlin, M. E. 1999. Controlling method effects in self-report instruments. Research methods division, Academy of Management. Available: http://www.aom.pace.edu/rmd/1999_RMD_Forum_Method_Effects_in_Self-Reports.htm [Accessed 2001].

Morris, P. W. G., and G. H. Hough. 1987. *The Anatomy of Major Projects.* London: John Wiley and Sons Inc.

Munns, A. K., and B. F. Bjeirmi. 1996. The role of project management in achieving project success. *International Journal of Project Management* 14 (2): 81–88.

OnTarget. 1999. Sales Management Best Practices. Philidelphia, PA: OnTarget Inc.

Pfeffer, J., and R. I. Sutton. 2000. *The Knowing Doing Gap: How Smart Companies Turn Knowledge into Action,* 1st ed. Boston: Harvard Business School Press.

Pinto, J. K., and J. G. Covin. 1989. Critical factors in project implementation: A comparison study of construction and R&D projects. *Technovation* 9 (1): 49–51.

Pinto, J. K., and S. J. J. Mantel. 1990. The causes of project failure. *IEEE Transactions on Engineering Management* 37 (4): 269–277.

Pinto, J. K., and J. E. Prescott. 1990. Planning and tactical factors in project implementation success. *The Journal of Management Studies* 27 (3): 305–328.

Pinto, J. K., and D. P. Slevin. 1987. Critical factors in successful project implementation. *IEEE Transactions on Engineering Management* EM34 (1): 22–28.

———. 1988a. Critical success factors across the project life cycle. *Project Management Journal* 19 (3): 67–75.

———. 1988b. Project success: Definitions and measurement techniques. *Project Management Journal* 19 (1): 67–73.

———. 1989. Critical success factors in R&D projects. *Research Technology Management* 32 (1): 31–36.

Project Management Institute. 2000. *A Guide to the Project Management Body of Knowledge (PMBOK® Guide)* – 2000 Edition. Newtown Square, PA: Project Management Institute.

Price, C. R. 1999. *Creating Rainmakers: The Manager's Guide to Training Professionals*, Vol. 10: Book review.

Reynolds, P. D. 1971. *A Primer in Theory Construction*, 1st Ed. New York: MacMillan Publishing Company/Collier MacMillan Publishing.

Rockhart, J. J., and J. E. Short. 1991. The networked organization and the management of interdependence. In M. S. Scott-Morton (Ed.), *The Corporation of the 1990s—Information Technology and Organizational Transformation*. New York: Oxford University Press.

Sawy, E., A. Malhotra, S. Gosain, and K. Young. 1999. IT-intensive value innovation in the electronic economy: Insights from Marshall Industries. *MIS Quarterly* 23 (3): 305–333.

Schlichter, J. 1999. Surveying project management capabilities (*PM Network*). Available: http://www.pmi.org/standards/pmcapabilities.html [Accessed 2000].

Scolari. 1997. ATLAS- ti qualitative software analysis software.

SEI. 2001. SEI capability maturity models. Carnegie Mellon University. Available: http://www.sei.cmu.edu [Accessed 2001].

Shaw, M. L. G., and B. R. Gaines. 1995. Comparing conceptual structures: Consensus, conflict, correspondence and contrast. Knowledge Science Institute, University of Calgary, Alberta, Canada. Available: http://ksi.cpsc.ucalgary.ca/articles/KBS/COCO/ [Accessed 2001].

Shenhar, A. J., O. Levy, and D. Dvir. 1997. Mapping the dimensions of project success. *Project Management Journal* 28 (2): 5–13.

SISA. 1989. Simple interpretive statistical analysis. Available: http://home.clara.net/sisa/resprhlp.htm.

Standish. 1996. The CHAOS report: Unfinished voyages. The Standish Group. Available: http://standishgroup.com/visitor/chaos.htm [Accessed March 2001].

———. 2001. The extreme chaos report: Unfinished voyages. Standish Group. Available: http://standishgroup.com/visitor/chaos.htm.

Strauss, A. L., and J. Corbin. 1990. *Basics of Qualitative Research: Grounded Theory Procedures and Techniques*. Thousand Oaks, CA: Sage Publications.

Sutton, R. I., and B. M. Staw. 1995. What theory is not. *Administrative Science Quarterly* 40 (3): 371–384.

Thomas, J. 2000. Making Sense of Project Management. Unpublished PhD Dissertation, University of Alberta, Edmonton.

Thomas, J., C. Delisle, and K. Jugdev. 2002a, July. Getting Senior Executives on Side or Selling Project Management to Executives: Phase II. Paper presented at Project Management Institute Research Conference 2002 in Seattle, Washington, USA.

———. 2002b. *Selling Project Management to Senior Executives: Monograph*, 1st Ed. Vol. 1. Newtown Square, PA: Project Management Institute.

Thomas, J., C. Delisle, K. Jugdev, and P. Buckle. 2000a, June. Selling Project Management to Senior Executives—What's the Hook? Paper presented at Project Management Institute Research Conference in Paris, France.

———. 2000b, October. Selling Project Management to Executives. Paper presented at Project Management Institute Syminar & Symposium in Houston, Texas.

———. 2001a. Mission Possible: Selling project management to senior executives. *PM Network* 15 (1): 59–62.

———. 2001b, November. Selling Project Management Research Study—Phase II. Paper presented at the Project Management Institute Seminar & Symposium in Nashville, Tennessee.

———. 2001c. Selling project management to senior executives: The case for avoiding crisis sales. *Project Management Journal* 33 (2): 19–28.

Turner, D., and M. Crawford. 1994. Managing current and future competitive performance: The role of competence. In G. Hamel and A. Heene (Eds.), *Competence-Based Competition* (pp. 241–263). Chichester: John Wiley & Sons, Inc.

Urli, B., and D. Urli. 2000. Project management in North America, stability of the concepts. *Project Management Journal* 31 (3): 33–43.

Ward, S., L. Light, and J. Goldstine. 1999. What high-tech managers need to know about brands. *Harvard Business Review*: 85–99.

Weible, R., and J. Wallace. 1998, Fall. Cyber research: The impact of the Internet on data collection. *Marketing Research* 10 (3).

Weick, K. E. 1995. What theory is not, theorizing is. *Administrative Science Quarterly* 40 (3): 385–390.

———. 1996. *SenseMaking*. CA: Sage Publications.

Weitz, B. A., and K. D. Bradford. 1999. Personal selling and sales management: A relationship marketing perspective. *Academy of Marketing Science* 27 (2): 241–254.